D1357598

The Deep End

The Deep End

A Memoir of Growing Up

Mary Rose Callaghan

UNIVERSITY OF DELAWARE PRESS
Newark

Published by University of Delaware Press
Copublished by The Rowman & Littlefield Publishing Group, Inc.
4501 Forbes Boulevard, Suite 200, Lanham, Maryland 20706
www.rowman.com

Unit A, Whitacre Mews, 26-34 Stannary Street, London SE11 4AB

British Library Cataloguing in Publication Information Available

Library of Congress Cataloging-in-Publication Data

Library of Congress Cataloging-in-Publication Data Available

ISBN 978-1-61149-622-2 (cloth : alk. paper)
ISBN 978-1-61149-623-9 (electronic)

∞™ The paper used in this publication meets the minimum requirements of American National Standard for Information Sciences Permanence of Paper for Printed Library Materials, ANSI/NISO Z39.48-1992.

Printed in the United States of America

Remembering my parents.

Our simple childhood sits upon a throne
That hath more power than all the elements.
——William Wordsworth, *The Prelude*, Book V

There is life before knowledge, and somebody before words. And every life is constituted through the generations that precede it, like an obscured inheritance.
——Adam Phillips, *Terrors and Experts*

Contents

Acknowledgments

Although I have changed some names for privacy, this is a work of nonfiction. Early versions of parts have appeared in *Confessions of a Prodigal Daughter*, *A Woman's Christmas*, and on RTÉ's Sunday Miscellany. Thanks to my siblings for allowing me to raid our childhood; to Web writing workshop for listening to early drafts; and to Brigid O'Brien for first suggesting a piece on homelessness. Thanks also to Martin Roper, Ivy Bannister, and Rachel Weiss; to all in the Ballsbridge Writing Group; to Maryanne Felter, Jeanne Murray Walker, Eilís Ní hAnluin, Adrian Kenny, Jennifer Fitzgerald, Rosemarie Rowley, Mairide Woods, Louise C. Callaghan, and Patrick Quill for reading first drafts. A special thanks to Kate Danaher for suggestions and editing. Thanks also to Faber & Faber, and to Lutyens & Rubinstein for permission to quote from Adam Phillips, to Una Sealy RHA for the cover, to the University of Delaware Press and Rowman & Littlefield for accepting the book, and to my agent, Jonathan Williams.

Prologue

Swimming is like life: you have to go in the deep end, or you can't float. After my family moved to Dún Laoghaire, it became our main summer activity. I took my younger siblings to the public baths, or we trooped off like the Famous Five to Sandycove strand, which cost nothing. As the eldest girl, I was in charge and we spent the day in the water, or building sandcastles when the tide was out. James Joyce's Martello Tower was nearby, and although I'd heard of our famous writer by then, I preferred Agatha Christie or Georgette Heyer. Still we often went round to the tower, or to the Forty Foot bathing place, to peep at the strutting, naked, "gentlemen-only" bathers. Women were prohibited from the best swimming place in Dublin then, and the ban existed until recently.

One day my parents came with us. My mother, an agency night nurse, was probably between jobs; my father was unemployed. By now they'd had famous, plate-throwing rows, and my one dread was my mother leaving my father. But they must have called a temporary truce. A hot spell had hit Ireland, the kind that happens once in a decade, and the memory is seared in my brain with its sun, salt water, shrieking children, and blue, blue sea. My mother lay with us on the sand by the rocks, looking uncomfortable in the heat. My father sat on the wall, peacefully smoking his pipe and reading the racing results. I had never seen him wear shorts and he didn't then. As usual, he was dressed elegantly in an ecru linen jacket and open-necked shirt, with flannel slacks. The tide was in, and water lapped enticingly at the sea wall.

"I'm going for a swim," my mother announced suddenly. Although an American, she had a mid-Atlantic accent that was not all that noticeable. At the time she was thirty-nine or forty with a slim figure and a look of Lady Lavery, the woman on the Irish pound note. She had dark, permed hair and pale Celtic skin. Unlike other émigrés, she didn't complain of the Irish weather, and always said she hated the sun. When we went for a dip in long childhood summers, she never joined us in the water. While my father watched over us, I remember her sitting on the rug, surrounded by buckets and spades, sun cream, the clutter of a picnic, a book in hand. She was a ferocious reader, but would towel us dry when we had run shrieking and shivering from the cruel Irish Sea.

I didn't know she could swim. She didn't even own togs, but wiggled into mine, borrowing my white bathing cap. I thought she might manage a pathetic dog paddle like everyone else did in those days, but, without any fuss, she dived from the wall and swam off in a strong graceful crawl. I was stunned. Where had she learned to swim properly? And dive without splashing for God's sake? My mother had a mind furnished with quotes from poetry and the Bible. "Throw your bread on the water" was a favorite. Now she was throwing herself on it. As she disappeared out to sea, I watched worriedly. Would she ever come back? She was a bad asthmatic, and the water might be too cold for her.

"Do you think she'll be OK?" I asked my father, who appeared beside me.

He stared at the sea. "Jesus."

Difficult as their marriage was, he didn't want to lose her. They were chained together like Paolo and Francesca, the hopeless lovers in Dante. He puffed on his pipe, then cupped it in his hand as he called her name.

But she couldn't hear. We both ran around to the Forty Foot—that way we could see better. From the other side of the wall, the two of us watched her shoulder the waves. It was pointless to call out again, as the white cap bobbed towards the horizon, far from other timid huggers of the shore. I had never seen anyone swim like that, except Johnny Weissmuller as Tarzan on our snowy TV. If she got asthma now, who would save her?

It was a long wait. But half an hour later my mother climbed up the steps, onto the sea wall. "The water's lovely. You should get in, darling!"

I stood there, as she toweled herself dry. "Are you OK?"

"Of course!" she laughed, dripping wet. "Don't look so worried."

My mother always told me not to worry. But I did, especially that one day she might be gone. After spats with my father, she regularly packed a suitcase and moved into a hotel, threatening to leave him permanently. It always filled me with panic. But that day was an oasis in time: a once-only, because I never saw her swim again. As she got dressed, I knew that you can never know anyone—not even your own mother. Everyone has a secret self, and she had lived another life before her children were ever thought of. A glamorous life—that I hoped to copy one day—of Florida beaches, endless boyfriends and, later, Atlantic voyages back and forth from New York to Cobh. She had even flown in one of those terrifying sea planes and landed at Foynes in County Kerry—before the trap of marriage.

Asthma is a frightening disease. Fear of my mother's attacks stalked my childhood. Sometimes they hit with the force of a panther, knocking the air from her lungs. When she started wheezing, there would be frantic searching for her big black inhaler, which was always getting lost in a haphazard house with six children. This usually happened inconveniently in the middle of the night when she ran out of medication. As I got older, it was my job to ring the doctor. On one occasion he had recommended steam inhalations.

"What are they?" I asked.

"*In-hal-ations*," he repeated into the receiver, yawning. "Your mother will know . . . boil a kettle, insert a plug in the sink, pour in the hot water. Then cover her head with a towel and get her to breathe in deeply."

"That won't work. She's dying."

He sent an ambulance.

It was an exaggeration, but I couldn't watch her gasping until the chemist opened in the morning. I don't know why she got asthma. It might have been the damp Irish climate. Although born in Dublin in 1918, she had sailed to New York as a toddler with her Irish-American father and two siblings after her mother's death the next year. The story goes that a nurse had tried to throw her overboard on the way, believing a motherless child would be better off dead. But she survived, and after the stock market crash of 1929 rode in the rumble seat of a Ford Model T with her family to Florida, escaping the Great Depression. She spent her teenage years there, and somehow this unconventional upbringing had rubbed off on us, because my sisters and I were known as "the Americans" in school—probably because we ate popcorn, or wore American hand-me-downs. But we thought of ourselves as Irish. After all, our mother had chosen this country. "When I'm eighteen, I'm going back to Ireland," she told everyone in Florida and, after her father's death in the mid-1930s, returned with his body in the ship's hold. He had wanted to be buried beside his wife in Glasnevin Cemetery. It was an exotic history.

Neuroscientists say that we don't have real memories: every time we recall something, we embellish it, adding or subtracting information. So a particular memory is a mish-mash: the memory of a memory. But I'm not so sure. There are some things we can never forget. In my case it was living in Dún Laoghaire. I was sandwiched between two brothers, then away at school. I had been a boarder too, but had left because my parents could no longer afford the high fees. My father had recently sold his farm, so the future was uncertain. But Dún Laoghaire had promised a better life. There were new schools to try, a pier with a brass band, cinemas, and a library. And, best of all, the sea. All roads led to it, and it changed color according to the weather.

My mother was full of stories. "I'm telling you this to help you with your writing," she'd say, launching into some incident from her youth. Or she would say, “Let’s analyze it,” when something happened in our family, or we met a strange character. It was great training. I was to be the writer in the family, but had no idea what to write about. I wasn’t even good at writing because I had missed a lot of school by then, but my mother told me that the unexamined life wasn’t worth living, and often quoted from a poem:

Dust thou art, to dust returnest,
Was not spoken of the soul.

Later I discovered the lines were by Longfellow, and that Socrates was the first to mention the unexamined life.

Chapter One

I am gripping the cot rails, as the door opens and my mother comes into the nursery with Bernie, who is to be our new nanny. Like all my early memories, this is a pop-up in a picture book, which always remains with me. We lived at the time in 4 Iona Park, Glasnevin, on Dublin's north side, which my parents had bought before my birth. It was a big red-bricked house, double-fronted and detached, solidly middle-class. Looking at it today, I know it must have been hard work to run. There were three reception rooms downstairs, with the kitchen down steps from a dark hall. The upstairs was spacious, although I remember the bedrooms only as closed doors, and that I was as tall as a vase on the landing.

My parents were married in 1941 on my father's birthday, October 29, a month before America entered the war. In Ireland the "Emergency" was in full swing. Dublin's North Strand had been bombed in error that year, and everyone feared that Ireland would be dragged into the conflict. But we escaped, thanks to de Valera's ensuring our neutrality. Still, thousands of Irish fought for the Allies, and at home there was food, petrol, and gas rationing. Although the gas was turned off, my mother told me that enough remained in the pipes to boil a kettle. This led to the "glimmerman," a gas company official peeping into windows to detect the blue glow. Despite hardships, life was cheerful: sales of bicycles soared in the war years, and my parents had carefree times cycling around the city. The Phoenix Park was called "the New Bog Road" because turf was piled along the main thoroughfare, and many Dubliners tended allotments to grow their own vegetables.

There was alarm about my mother's health then. Fear was in the air, which I sensed but didn't understand. Asthma specialists were called to the house, and she had almost died of a breech birth with Barry, who was born thirteen months after me. It was a near-death experience, with a figure appearing at the end of a long white tunnel. Everything had seemed clear to her.

"I couldn't wait to tell Daddy," she said. "I'd found the key to a puzzle."

There were three of us by then: my elder brother Maurice, me, and Barry. My brothers didn't seem to be in the nursery when Bernie came that day. So perhaps Maurice had his own room, but Barry might have been asleep in another cot. As a toddler, I had contracted some skin disease, so all my hair was shaved off and I look oddly modern in baby photographs from the time.

The day Bernie came my mother picked me up, smiling. Bernie smiled too; she always smiled around my parents. In my memory, her eyes are a cold blue behind round 1950s glasses, but I couldn't have noticed coldness then—that must be a later memory. She was a toothy girl with a ruddy, country face and short curly brown hair. While she stood in the background, my mother played with me for a few minutes, before kissing me goodnight. My mother was all gaiety then: everyone loved her, and I did especially. She was in her late twenties, and probably Bernie's senior by a decade.

Bernie was replacing two cheerful live-in maids, sisters, whom I remember vaguely. During their watch, my pram had upended, and I fell headfirst onto the pavement. I was concussed and my minders were afraid to tell my mother, but later they brought me into the drawing room and confessed.

"The doctor sedated you for twenty-four hours," my mother said.

While my father went out and got tight, she kept me in their double bed with the blue flowered spread. My father had done this before, but now she knew what was wrong. "The first time Daddy was drunk, I called the doctor," she said, laughing, years later. "I had never seen anyone intoxicated." Although her relatives disapproved of his drinking, there was no support for my mother leaving my father. It was unheard of for a marriage to end in the Ireland of that day. You made your bed and then lay on it.

I recovered, with no ill effects, although the two sisters left.

Bernie got the nanny's job and moved in and out of our lives until I was a teenager. While she fades into the background, I have other pop-up flashes of our time in Glasnevin. One is of running around the back garden with Maurice, and being as tall as the ferns growing there. Later, rag curlers are put in my hair and I'm staring into a mirror, wondering how to get inside: *Through the Looking Glass* must have been read to me, so this desire became a metaphor for the artistic endeavor.

My mother never allowed her children to fight, and insisted we make up any quarrel, reciting, like the three musketeers, "One for all and all for one." My father's family didn't get on and she feared the same would happen to us. She was to have three more children, two girls and another boy. Although the marital bed was policed by the Catholic Church, it was her own decision to continue having children, she later told me. She wasn't religious, but she wanted a big family: six was average at the time. Although I have the blessing of sisters and brothers, it was hard on my mother's health.

In the bitter winter of 1947, when Ireland was snowbound, my mother made a joke of it, telling me that she kept us children in bed and fed us on raisins, because it was impossible to go shopping. During the bus strike of that year, Maurice got lost in town and was brought home by a teenage boy. I have a mental picture of them getting out of an army truck and walking hand-in-hand into the house, but whether this is an actual memory or something I was later told about, I don't know.

I do remember going to the Botanic Gardens daily with my mother or Bernie, and spending the afternoons running around the huge glasshouses with their tropical atmosphere and pungent smell of damp geraniums, or rolling down a grassy hill. One day Maurice broke his leg outside Players' cigarette factory and ended up in a plaster cast. Glasnevin was the limits of our world, although we did go to Lahinch in County Clare on my first holiday, and I have memory flashes of sand dunes and trying to tie my bootlaces. Then Auntie Ellen, my mother's older sister, flew all the way from Florida and landed at Shannon in one of the early planes. I remember her giving me a gift—a blue wooden horse—and, later, trying to keep up, as she strode across the churchyard to collect Maurice from the nearby national school. My mother was delighted by her sister's visit because they hadn't seen each other since before the war, and there was a round of parties, although the holiday ended in tears. There's a photograph of my parents seeing my aunt off at the airport; my mother is in obvious distress and being consoled by my father. There was a dispute about a camera, which my aunt had brought from the States at his request, I heard later. But it must have been something more: I suspect there was tension because my mother seemed happier than my aunt, who was exiled in Florida, far from her dead mother's country. It shows you can never trust appearances.

Bernie always put us to bed early, but even as a young child, I found falling asleep difficult. I remember hearing a song in my cot: "Goodnight, Irene. I'll see you in my dreams." Who is Irene? Will she come to my dreams? A boy on the road is called Jackie McNamara and there is a song for him too, "McNamara's Band."

My name is McNamara, I'm the leader of the band
And though we're small in number, we're the best in all the land.

One afternoon, I look through a window and see my father in the front garden, waving to me. I run out to him. His shaven face, smelling of tobacco, whiskey, and soap, tickles mine when he kisses me. He calls me his "Queen" . . . and I love him more than anyone.

Life was happy at first for my parents. Imbibing was tolerated by society, for men at least—a drunken woman was another matter. My father was a farmer who lived in town. He was into racehorses, greyhounds, golf, religion, and drink. The Benjamin of his family, he was the indulged afterthought of wealthy parents. His cattle-dealer father, dead for some years, had left a thousand acres of fully stocked land. His mother, reputedly of French Huguenot origin, was dead too. In 1916, when the Easter Rising started, my father was nine years old and at Fairyhouse races with his father. Because the family wasn't political, the event was ignored. According to family myth, my paternal grandfather hadn't seen his own father until aged ten, owing to some political involvement, and this had entrenched the family's neutrality. Making money was the important thing for them so, on growing up, my father had chauffeured his own father around Ireland, in an era when cars were rare.

Now he went to fairs alone on black market petrol, buying cattle which he fattened and then sold on to abattoirs or at the Dublin Cattle Market, which always took place on a Wednesday morning when live cattle were herded up from the country. But the beef business required capital, always scarce for my father. It was the middle of Ireland's economic war with Britain, so times were bad for all farmers, because of tariffs on exports. The thirties had been a hard decade and, with the ongoing economic war, the future looked no better.

While my father traveled the country, my mother looked after the house. It was her job to cook the meals, take care of us, and look pretty. From being a Florida orphan, she had reinvented herself and enjoyed her new status and beautiful home. The curtains and upholstery, with their strong blues and oranges, lasted well into my childhood. Her dead mother's family had been generous with wedding gifts. "We had a house full of antiques," she told me. Middle-class married women didn't usually work outside the home, but still housework was a problem for my mother. In those years she had a weekly charlady, as well as one or two maids. Domestic drudgery was one of the few jobs available to a small farmer's daughter like Bernie. It was slavery really. Whatever difficulties we have run into in post–Celtic Tiger Ireland, the young are now educated and can go to college or to apprenticeships.

In the 1940s my mother was thought to be crazy for paying a girl a pound a week: the going rate was less, fifteen shillings plus board, she told me later. Coming from democratic America, she was amazed at the meanness of the neighborhood wives who could afford to pay more. They spent their lives bringing up children and "talking about the price of tomatoes"; it was the culture of the time. The Irish Constitution protected a wife's position in the home. The famous "bar," which required Irish female civil servants to give up their jobs on marriage, lasted into the 1970s and percolated down to most other professions except teaching. Jobs were for men, women were childbearers. There might have been occasional bridge parties and sales of work to attend, but on the whole women were condemned to drudgery. Yet housework wasn't even considered real work. Men were the breadwinners and more important. Although they might cut the grass, they usually did nothing in the house except maybe put on the kettle, which was my father's habit on returning from the Sunday drives of my childhood. In later years he would give me lessons on how to make tea properly: boil fresh water, heat the teapot, use one teaspoon of tea per person, and one for the pot.

I loved having tea parties with my dolls. And everything about us as babies fascinated me. Maurice's birth had been hard, but I had come on the dot and without pain, my mother said. Because new mothers stayed in bed for longer then, my christening had been attended by my father, his elder sister, who was my godmother, and my mother's cousin Eileen. My mother, who had a penchant for exotic names, had wanted to call me Griselda, but, thanks to my father's intervention, settled for "Mary Rose," which her cousin thought unlucky: the fairies would woo me away, as in the J. M. Barrie play of the same name. So, on her insistence, my father changed it to "Mary Frances" which ended up on my birth certificate, although I have never used it. "Mary" was for the Virgin, and "Frances" used for four of us children to commemorate the grandfather who had left all the land. My father had loved his father, but not his mother. To me it seemed unfair, so, years later, I took her name, Anne, for my confirmation.

My parents didn't seem to have many visitors, although Auntie Bronwyn, my mother's best friend, did come occasionally. I seem to remember her visits, but probably they are a later memory. She was a slim and elegant medical student, with short hair and a bell-like English public school accent. For years I had a silver napkin ring, engraved *Mary Rose*, her christening present, which must have been stolen or lost, because I don't have it now. Auntie Bronwyn was a woman many men were in love with, but she had avoided marriage, refusing a long-time suitor. One day she disappeared and married him, without telling my parents. It was a mystery.

We were well-off then with two cars: a station wagon and a gray sports MG with a silver bull mascot on the bonnet. My mother didn't drive, but would take the bus to town. One day after her shopping, she was planning to go on to a party in Uncle Ted's house—our father's older brother lived nearby on the North Circular Road—but she got the wrong bus by mistake and ended up at home. It was just as well, she told me later: now she could kiss her children goodnight. She went into the nursery where Barry felt limp in her arms. Something wasn't right, so she told our nanny to call the doctor. This is ridiculous, she told herself on the way to her party at Uncle Ted's: you can't worry about every little thing.

But a phone message was waiting at my uncle's house. The doctor had just finished his training, so he recognized the symptoms of diphtheria. "Baby Bar," as we called my brother, spent the next few months in Cork Street Hospital, and my mother visited him there every day, bringing a rattle each time. When he returned home the rattles had to be left behind in the fever hospital, but her intuition had saved my brother's life.

Everything looked good for my parents, and I had a fortunate early childhood. Bernie was efficient and highly valued, but, along with my father's drinking, she is the other dark thread in the tapestry. Although they didn't always do it themselves, middle-class parents at the time allowed nannies to beat their children. Around this time Bernie started physically punishing me. Corporal punishment was widespread and common in Irish schools too, although it happened mainly to boys. It wasn't a good time for children's rights anywhere.

Chapter Two

I was four when my parents moved south across the city to 34 Merton Drive, Ranelagh. It was for financial reasons, I learned later, and I remember waiting with Bernie in the empty house, while she unpacked tea chests full of crockery: we must have come ahead to let in the movers. The house, although in a good neighborhood, was a smaller semi-detached, so some of the furniture wouldn't fit and had to be auctioned off on the Liffey quays. This move was a foreshadowing of times to come, but my mother was good at letting things go, and we weren't the only family in difficulties. Tuberculosis was rife at the time. There was unemployment and mass emigration from the countryside, and wartime rationing remained. Being Irish, I never think of myself as a war baby but of course I am, and I do remember queuing with my mother for sugar rations in the 1950s.

At that time, my mother told me where babies came from. It was something to do with gardening. "God plants a seed in the mother's heart," she said. "Then the doctor comes and takes it away."

"I thought it was in your *room,*" I said.

She laughed. "My room?"

It was in the Hail Mary. "Blessed is the fruit of thy room, Jesus."

"It's *womb*. Thy *womb*, Jesus."

"Womb" was a new word. Did I have one too? I must, if Mammy did. Later on we called her "Mummy," because she thought the Irish "Mammy" was a demeaning term for black women in Florida, where she had grown up.

By now my parents had four children, two boys and two girls. My sister Olwyn, whose Welsh name was suggested by my mother's best friend, had been born, and another sister, Evie, was on the way. Iona Park had been sold for four thousand pounds, a fortune at the time. My mother's inheritance had paid for it, but the banks were now pressing my father for debts. The war was over but he still hadn't enough capital to invest in cattle. Like many farmers at the time, he was land rich but cash poor. Still, the house sale would provide him with funds—things were bound to improve.

There were only three bedrooms in our new home. My parents had the biggest, Maurice, who was delicate, had the box-room, and the rest of us slept in the nursery with Bernie, which must have been hell for her. I remember her dressing to go out on her weekly night off, while we were meant to be asleep. On one of those occasions, Barry and I were left alone in the nursery, but instead of sleeping, entertained ourselves by climbing out of one windows, walking along the sill, and coming in another, escaping a fall onto a concrete patio. We had no sense of danger, but luckily a neighbor alerted my mother. She ran into the room, not angry but relieved that we were unhurt.

Bernie had total charge of us, giving us meat and potatoes for midday dinner and jam or banana sandwiches for tea. Sometimes we had cereal, and I remember thinking the cornflakes in my bowl were the land and the milk the sea, which I would cross one day. Every Saturday night we got a neat pile of clean clothes and, during Lent, Bernie brought us to daily Mass, which was endlessly boring. The afternoons when we went to Herbert Park, a child holding onto each side of the pram as Bernie pushed the new baby, were more enjoyable. We played by the duck pond for hours, sailing boats or fishing for frog-spawn or pinkies, which we brought home in jam jars and left in the bathroom until they died. I don't remember when Bernie's beatings started or ended. As a young child, I wet myself and she severely punished me for this. She was cold and ritualistic and would threaten me all the way home from the park, then pull me, naked, out of the nightly bath and apply the clothes brush, which really hurt. If it were raining, I escaped, presumably because my pants might be wet from the weather. Even then I thought this illogical—how could rain get through my outer clothes?

Children have a sense of justice—a punishment must be fair. Still, I don't think of myself as a victim—not compared to the abuse of children in Irish orphanages, which has recently come to light. But it was bad psychology, as it is now well known that childhood wetting is caused by anxiety. I assume my mother knew nothing about Bernie's behavior, but I never asked her when I got older because she had enough problems. She sometimes lost her temper with us, but rarely. Later on I was shocked to hear her say that she dreaded traveling by bus with us, because we were so wild. Wild? Us? I had always thought, probably wrongly, that although she'd had a hard life, we made up for it, but child-rearing is hard work. In our early years she was an attentive and loving mother, reading us stories as we fell asleep in the nursery with the electric fire glowing. I don't remember learning to read myself. Aunt Noreen—another of our few visitors and my mother's older first cousin, whom we always called "aunt," and who was to be important in our lives—told me that I could read the newspaper at age three or four.

"I don't remember that," I said.

"Well, I do!"

Aunt Noreen was someone you didn't argue with. She assured me it was true, since I was ahead of her daughter, Niamh, in reading, who was a year older than me, and this worried her. We often met Aunt Noreen and her sisters in Bewley's Café, with its heavenly aroma of coffee, for tea and cakes. We had many distant relations whom my mother loved and who loved her, before her life got difficult.

I was about six when I awoke one night to see her sitting in the middle of the nursery, head bent and crying. The next thing my father burst in and doused her with cold water. She was perfectly sober, but he was blind drunk.

I looked in panic to Bernie, awake in the next bed. It was a rare moment of communication between us, because she put a finger silently to her lips, indicating that I should feign sleep. I froze with fear, but don't remember what happened next. Children were told nothing then. Years later, I asked my mother about it. "I went in there for safety," she explained. "I shouldn't have. But I thought Daddy wouldn't follow me."

My mother had taken his car keys to stop him from going out again. His life had become a cycle of binges. Once he woke up to find that he'd crashed his car in a ditch. Afterwards there were extended periods of repentant sobriety when he dragged us all off to daily Mass. While my mother wasn't conventionally religious and claimed, to my father's irritation, that she was an American Episcopalian, my father was a devout Irish Catholic. We regularly did the Nine First Fridays for a plenary indulgence and, during Holy Week, visited seven churches, according to Dublin tradition. At Halloween my father made us sweep up the nut shells from the drawing room carpet, in case the Holy Souls hurt their feet. I always wanted to wait up on this magical night when they visited from the other world.

One afternoon on the way to the park, we passed my mother at the Sandford Park school railings. The previous day there had been a bad row: she had put on her coat, packed her suitcase, and checked into a hotel, but my father had found her and somehow persuaded her to return. Now she was wearing sunglasses to hide a black eye.

I called to her but Bernie pulled me on, as my mother hurried homewards in the opposite direction with a male friend consoling her. He was the brother of a famous pianist, Jenny Reddin, I later learned. I had never seen him before, and this says something about my mother's isolation. My father had been caught having an affair. He had a habit of making a play for my mother's friends, but, when she complained to her cousins, she was told, "Your husband is devoted to you." A husband's infidelity was more acceptable than a wife's.

I wanted to make up for her black eye, so I started picking wild flowers for her through the Sandford Park railings on the way home from school. I had to make sure she didn't leave Daddy. What would become of us then?

But these worries usually receded, and there were happier times. My parents arranged all sorts of extracurricular lessons, for instance, elocution where I remember reciting tongue twisters to improve my diction: "Round the rugged rocks the ragged rascal ran." In another pop-up memory, I am standing on a stage, dressed as a playing card in an acting school's production of *Alice in Wonderland.* Upstage, Maurice, another card, stands amongst a group of glassy-eyed children. Somehow we have got inside Alice's looking glass, but staring out at the audience terrifies me. I had no acting talent, then or now.

Merton Drive was a lucky time. I made friends in school, also playing on the street—part of childhood then. My best friend was called "Specky-four-eyes" because she wore glasses, and I remember my mother explaining how unkind this nickname was. Another neighborhood boy's father was dead, which shocked me, and I was convinced that the body was buried under the pile of rocks in his garden. I realized that my parents would die one day. I would die, everyone would. But this fear was forgotten when the breadman's van, pulled by a horse, arrived daily and we enjoyed scary, clattering rides, sitting high up beside the driver. On foot we went farther, exploring the area as far as Palmerston Park, playing on the swings and see-saws there. For the first time I became aware of class distinctions, as hordes of poorer children from the Mount Pleasant Buildings yelled, "Yu-u-ung one, get outta me way!" knocking me to the ground.

Maurice went to St. Conleth's, a posh prep school, while I attended the Dominican convent at Muckross Park, which I loved. I was joined by Barry, and Olwyn was to follow when I was eight. On her first day she howled the place down and, when summoned, I squeezed into a small round-backed chair beside her.

"What's wrong?" I asked again and again, but she was inconsolable. I was the big sister, but could do nothing to comfort her. Loneliness was the human condition, like my fear of death.

For my First Communion, my mother and I went shopping in Cassidy's of Upper George's Street. She picked out a white-smocked Viyella dress, but I wanted a tasteless nylon long-sleeved one, like every other girl was wearing. When I insisted, she looked hurt, and that devastated me. Although I got my way, I'd have done anything to bring back the nylon dress. I wanted to please my mother and couldn't bear to see her unhappy. Her sorrows were my sorrows, which was some sort of codependence, I now realize. Later on, this made breaking away from her difficult.

One day she came into the nursery to say goodnight. She was crying, as she hugged us tightly, and said that she had been shopping in O'Connell Street when a man had jumped off Nelson's Pillar, committing "suicide." I repeated the new word to myself, wondering what sorrows could drive anyone to this. How could anyone want to die?

My father's business picked up and he started making money in the early 1950s. As one of Ireland's first meat exporters, he was part of a consortium of cattle buyers who shipped meat abroad. But the money went quickly. He bought a big black Chevrolet, which he let me steer on country roads while sitting on his lap in the driver's seat. At this time Maurice and I toured the Ring of Kerry with my parents—the Kerry accent sounded so strange, I thought it must be a foreign language. I got new clothes too—a maroon woolen dressing gown and matching fluffy slippers—to the amazement of the neighborhood. Children didn't have dressing gowns then, and slippers were a novelty. I had a few bought clothes but my summer frocks were made by a dressmaker, all gingham check from the same bolt. The summers must have been fine, if I could wear cotton.

My father had been brought up with horses, so Maurice and I began riding lessons in Dudgeon's School in what is now the University College Dublin campus in Belfield. We would walk there on Saturday mornings, and when I rode Rufus, a tame Connemara pony, through the woods, I imagined adventures on the American prairies. This was inspired by cowboy serials, or else scenes from *Black Beauty*, my favorite book. Maurice rode competitively in gymkhanas and in the Royal Dublin Society Spring Show on his own pony, Olivia. She was a stocky gray with mad blue eyes, and I later rode her too. She would take off with me aboard, circling the riding school arena, as the instructor, a hardy Scottish man, waited in silent fury. But pulling the reins was useless. I could do nothing but hang on until Olivia, eyes showing white, stopped suddenly of her own accord and sometimes threw me off.

My brothers and I walked to the Spring Show by ourselves, which would be unlikely to happen today—Bernie must have been on holidays, since we were unsupervised. We would set off each day and collect as many free samples as possible at the show. One year our dog, Trout, was stolen. He was a gentle Staffordshire bull terrier and his loss was a great sorrow. But there were other losses to come.

I saw my first films at this time: *Samson and Delilah*, with Hedy Lamarr and blind Victor Mature, who pulled down the temple with his bare hands; *The Boy with Green Hair*, starring Dean Stockwell as a bullied war orphan; and *Treasure Island* with a terrifying Robert Newton as Long John Silver. In Dublin's Metropole Cinema, with its liveried doormen, Bernie or my mother passed chocolates along the row to the three of us. On Saturdays we always went to the local matinée by ourselves, paying eight-pence for the balcony, while unruly and screaming foot-stampers filled the four-penny stalls—a class division of the time. This was an Aladdin's Cave of delights: a cliff-hanging *Flash Gordon* serial, a *Lone Ranger* short, and a longer "cowboy" picture. We came out blinking at the daylight and sick from fizz bags. Barry and I once bought a shop's entire supply with money we had won on the Aintree Grand National. My father had made us a bet of a shilling each way, to win or place. He often did this. With a previous winning of one pound, I had bought Maurice a kite.

Our family went on a yearly picnic to Ireland's Eye, a small island off Howth. This ritual meant hiring a boat and was a daylong adventure organized by my father. He also brought us for Sunday drives to the Wicklow mountains, or to Glendalough for afternoon tea in the hotel there. Sometimes we went to the Dublin Zoo, where we had elephant or pony rides or visited the urine-stinking lion and monkey houses. Every summer, he arranged annual holidays: my mother would have preferred to stay at home, but he rented houses, with outside toilets and big copper baths in the kitchen, for a month or sometimes three, where we spent our days building sandcastles or dipping in and out of the water. We usually went to Skerries, north of Dublin, but one year it was to a mouse-infested cottage in Rush, which we were compelled to leave. Another time we went to Brittas Bay in County Wicklow, where my doll was stolen on the beach. We always brought helpers, who supervised us, while our parents socialized in the pub or at the golf club. My mother didn't play, but my father had a decent handicap and was a member of Portmarnock Golf Club which, to this day, doesn't allow women full membership.

Summers in Skerries were spent wading out to an island, having adventures like children in books. We also attended evening fit-ups—plays performed by traveling companies or films shown on a wonky projector. On other evenings we rode on the bumpers and my father bought us candy floss. In one memory I have an earache and for some reason am alone in bed in a rental—called the Red House—while the rest of the family has gone somewhere. A motorbike rally roars terrifyingly outside, as I hide under the blankets. Then my mother runs into the room. "It's all right, darling, I'm here."

One year we went to a holiday camp for a change. It was an all-in vacation in County Meath, where you slept in a little chalet and swam in a big pool; usually students on holiday work looked after the children. It was fun for us and I learned another new word, "vacation." But it must have been hell for my parents. I can't imagine how they stuck through egg-and-spoon races and the false jollity of organized entertainment. The camp was full of English people, holidaying in postwar Ireland, before the tide changed and they went south to the Spanish sun.

Barry almost drowned in the swimming pool that year, and the ventriloquist, who entertained the children, took a fancy to me. He insisted that I sit beside him at the music-hall entertainments, and during the show, he put my hand on his private parts. To this day I remember his musty odor. In the dark I wondered why he was so rude, but was afraid to tell anyone. We were forbidden to talk to strangers, and this man wasn't a stranger. But the holiday must have been considered a success because we returned the next year. Again the ventriloquist and his horrible dummy singled me out for attention. I remember being alone in a chalet with him, and my mother running up the path, into the house, and grabbing me to safety. Did anything happen before she came? I don't remember.

It didn't occur to me that this special attention was abuse. But it must have disturbed me because one night, while we were there, I fell out of the top bunk, hurting my chin. I'd had a terrible nightmare that Barry had died in a fire and I couldn't save him. Everyone asked what the dream was about, but I was afraid to say in case he might actually die—to this day I am afraid of dreams. We had to leave the holiday camp early that year because Evie, then the baby at home, got scarlet fever and we were put into quarantine. So I escaped the pedophile. "I had my eye on him," my mother said years later. Today we wonder why child abuse seems to be everywhere. But it was always prevalent, although no one talked about it, especially the child in question, who usually thought that he or she had done something wrong. As a small child I had been put to bed without tea for hugging a bus conductor's legs. Would I also be blamed for the ventriloquist's interest in me?

As well as organizing holidays for us, my father went away by himself. He had gone skiing in his youth, to Berlin for the 1936 Olympic Games where he had seen Hitler. And in 1950 he had traveled to Rome for Holy Year with Auntie Bronwyn and a coachload of other pilgrims. My mother, suspecting nothing, encouraged him in this and she met him in London, on his way home, where they stayed in the Grosvenor House Hotel in Park Lane. It was their only break together since their honeymoon.

As a young child I bonded with my father. He always made me feel special in comparison to my brothers, and, when they went to boarding school, he brought me to school rugby matches. Although I had no interest in the game, I loved sitting in the stands beside him with a travel rug over my knee. Later on we saw Little Mo play tennis in Fitzwilliam Tennis Club, and I did develop an interest in that game. "I'm sending you to a finishing school in Switzerland," he often said, so I imagined an alpine future, in a school like the one in the Chalet books. When we drove to Dubber, his farm north of the city, we always passed through Mountjoy Square, Dublin's worst slum, full of tenements and barefoot children. Ragged boys swarmed around, begging to mind the car if my father stopped for any reason. Later I thought I'd imagined they had no shoes, but photographs of the time bear me out: Dublin was poor. There were chasms between the classes, and I felt overwhelmed by the plight of poor people. We were lucky to be so well-off.

At the farm we harnessed Olivia, which wasn't an easy task, as she was so frisky and mad. She was grazing in a field called the Lodge—all the fields in Irish farms have names. Then, while I rode around, my father checked on his greyhounds, housed in a shed; they were looked after by the workman who fed them on brown bread. Greyhounds were my father's hobby: one, Pasadena Beach, had been a winner and he hoped for another, as a way of making easy money. Later, as we walked the dogs over the fields, he called them with a high-pitched whistle, explaining that they had better hearing than humans. He had a feeling for nature and once showed me a fox's den with cubs, or, on another day, a water-hen's nest. He often bent down and picked a blade of grass. "A miracle," he said, holding it up. "It feeds cattle—Ireland's most important industry."

One day he pointed through the hedges at an old yellow-washed farmhouse. "We're going to live there someday," he said to me.

Chapter Three

Christmas is coming, the goose is getting fat,
Please put a penny in the old man's hat.
If you haven't got a penny, a ha'penny will do,
If you haven't got a ha'penny, God bless you!

Barry and I screamed the lines, as we jumped off a haycock. It was winter and the daylight hours were short. Santa Claus wasn't true, but it didn't matter: Christmas was coming, our first in the spooky dark. Rural electrification had taken place throughout Ireland, but the unlit country roads were still as black as death. Light came only from a nearby cottage, and the isolated house to which we had moved.

We had again zigzagged across the city, this time back from south to north. My father had finally bought Dubber House, a nineteenth-century farmhouse, along with fields adjoining our land, because the two properties had originally been one. It was his dream to bring us up in the country with plenty of fresh air. Also it was a safer place than the city, and, according to my father, if there were a nuclear war, we could build an air raid shelter. My mother had more mundane concerns: she was now stranded, since she didn't drive, and there weren't many buses to the city. It's hard to believe how rural north County Dublin was then. Although only a few miles from the city center, it was the country. Nearby Ballymun village, which is now part of Dublin city, was a parish church surrounded by a few cottages.

Dickens would have been proud of my parents. To be ready for Christmas they would start shopping in early November or even October, and about then a bulge would appear on top of the big wardrobe, and every time the poor innocents went out, we devious children would play with the new toys. The deception came to an end only when Barry pulled the wardrobe over, nearly killing himself. There were always extravagant presents under the tree: train sets, bikes, dolls. I got a doll's pram when I was six, and a nurse's uniform the next year.

"I'm going to be a nurse like you," I told my mother, as I walked around the house in my Red Cross apron, or played "doctors" with Barry.

"You can go to the Mater," she said, launching into one of her stories.

I never tired of hearing how unusual it was for an American to train in an Irish hospital in the late 1930s. It had been four years of hard work. When warned that, as a probationer, she would have to lay out dead bodies, my mother had retorted, "I want to justify my existence." One day she was introduced to a black doctor. They would never have shaken hands in Florida, she said, which seemed shocking to me, but she explained that that was why she liked Ireland better. Here a black man was considered a normal human being.

I recently met a Derry woman from the same nursing set, who described my mother's beautiful clothes and fashion sense. Although used to all mod cons, my mother had never complained about the Spartan conditions of the nurses' home—worse than boarding school and quite rigorous. The probationers slept in dormitories with no running water, just a pitcher and basin on the bedside locker. They rose at dawn and worked long hours in public wards.

My mother told me other things: of throwing a tray in protest at the inedible food; of getting into trouble for being "unkempt"—a single strand of hair was sticking out of her veil as she rushed on duty. She had a furious temper, concealing a gentle nature, yet, despite this, had made many friends in the Mater. When I grew up, I would make friends too, as well as help sick people. Maybe I wouldn't have to lay out dead bodies.

After we moved to the country, there was talk of my mother visiting family in America—she hadn't been back since her marriage—but that was postponed because all the money had been spent on Dubber House. It was comfortable, with thick walls, symmetrical windows, and a front porch, like a child's drawing. Two ground floor rooms took up the width of the house, and a dividing hall led to a downstairs bathroom, a maid's room, and a big kitchen overlooking an enclosed yard of ancient byres and sheds. There were four bedrooms upstairs and an annex—the sleeping quarters of laborers in past times—which became the playroom, and where we later put on entertainments for our parents. For months my father had had a builder renovate everything: digging the well, installing a huge Aga stove, painting and decorating the house, spending a fortune. I had my own bedroom with personally chosen silver-dotted wallpaper.

We children had more space now and in wet weather played 78 records on my father's turntable, housed in a big mahogany chest. He bought us a recording of *The Snow Goose* by Paul Gallico and *The Mikado* by Gilbert and Sullivan. The radio was usually on in the kitchen, and we heard *The*

Kennedys of Castleross on Radio Éireann and *Mrs. Dale's Diary* on the BBC. I always went to bed with Radio Luxembourg. "It's half-past nine and time for Perry Mason," the announcer would say in the flickering firelight—to this day, I often fall asleep with the radio on, which, for me, works like a pill. There is someone out there and I am not alone.

"On a little by-road, out beyant Finglas, he was found" is a quote from *Juno and the Paycock* by Sean O'Casey, but it describes the remoteness of our farm. It was in the middle of flat grass and tillage fields, where the only visitor was the breadman in a van. Dublin Airport was nearby and the odd rumbling airplane, flying low over the house, the only noise. Cottages were clustered around Dubber Cross at the top of the lane where people still drew water from a pump. The lane stopped at our gate, then an overgrown laurel avenue led to the house which stood in the middle of woodland trees. The yard was hidden behind big gates, and white railings surrounded the front gravel. A tennis hard-court had been built in the front paddock, a relic of better days, but it had cracked by this time, and it was a job to keep down the weeds. And the housework must have been even harder for my mother, who had a sixth child on the way. In my father's photographs of the time, she looks worn out.

In the pitch black nights, it took all my courage to ignore the ghosts in the surrounding countryside. While I had dismissed Santa Claus, I believed in a spirit world. North County Dublin was an ancient place, and St. Patrick was believed to have stopped there on his journey through Ireland. According to Catholic dogma, I had a guardian angel, so the existence of leprechauns and fairies was equally believable, as there were ring forts in the area. My father, a gifted storyteller, said the devil often appeared as a black dog, or as a man with cloven hooves, so I found myself looking at the workman's shoes. The house was meant to be haunted, too, by the previous owner, a woman who drank disinfectant in mourning for a dead baby.

In daylight the ghosts subsided, and the mist-covered fields were wonderful for roaming with the dogs. There was Jock, the retarded Kerry Blue, and Spot, the clever mongrel. They chased the neighbors' sheep, and we frantically caught up with them all the live-long day. In summer we helped make the hay and got rides on the buggy. My two brothers and I cycled for miles by ourselves, sometimes as far as Ashbourne, a nearby village. Or else we took the bus into town for the pictures: there were only a few buses daily, so if you missed one, you were stranded. When we first moved, my father arranged a taxi account with Archer's garage in Finglas and made us memorize our phone number—341110. Later, when funds dried up, we got the bus to Finglas and walked the extra miles home to Dubber. The road, although poetically named Watery Lane, was a long trudge.

For the first months in Dubber, I was in bed with hepatitis, probably picked up in school. It was lucky in a way, because I discovered the joy of reading alone: *Anne of Green Gables*, *Anne of Avonlea*, *What Katy Did*, and *Little Women* were all signed "Love, Daddy" in his copperplate hand—he always used expensive Parker pens. When recovered, I built a house out of orange crates in one of the trees and imagined myself a character from *The Children of the New Forest*. Or I would sit for hours on a homemade swing, hanging from one of the gnarled crabapple trees in the kitchen garden beside the house. It was before television reached Ireland, so children had to entertain themselves.

Auntie Bronwyn visited us again, wearing her elegant mink coat, and bringing Spangles and Mars Bars from the North of Ireland, where she lived. In her English accent, she admired my mother's tasteful new curtains and slipcovers. We loved her visits, as the sweets were unavailable in the south. "Auntie Bronwyn says you're the prettiest little girl she's ever seen," my mother said. I didn't see myself as pretty, but I knew girls had to be. Auntie Bronwyn was pretty; so was my mother.

Bernie had left by us now, to my great relief. We had other live-in help, as well as Delia Kelly, the charlady, who came out by bus on Saturdays. She had worked for us as long as I could remember, tidying the house, scrubbing the pine kitchen table with Vim, and making scones for tea which almost broke our teeth. But we all loved the kind, old-world countrywoman with the single strand of hair wrapped carefully around a bald patch. She called me "Miss Mary," as if I were a character from a Frances Hodgson Burnett novel. Her nephew was older than us and she talked about him nonstop.

Even though we lived on a farm, we weren't proper farmers. Most of the land was rented out for grazing, and our few animals were more of a hobby for my father. My mother grew vegetables for the house, and my father had a Jersey cow to supply us with milk. He even set up a churn to make butter. We had pigs with Christian names, and chickens. I had charge of the day-old chicks and loved watching the cheeping, fluffy-yellow bundles cuddle into each other under the heat lamp. As I got older, I was often sent by bus to buy their food from a special grain shop on the Dublin quays. Once, when the chicks had grown up, my mother turned them into American southern fried chicken, a recipe from her youth that I refused to eat. She was puzzled, but would she eat her children? I had a pet rabbit too, and one day brought it to the vegetable patch for lunch. When the savage tomcat appeared and dragged it off, I ran away, terrified. For years I regretted my cowardice: I should have tried to save my pet.

The workman lived in a farm cottage and earned four pounds a week with free board and milk. He was always threatening to catch us and "tan" our "backsides." Because he never caught us, nothing happened, but it was an odd thing to say. When my mother ordered him to do the weeding, my father told her not to interfere. This ended in a row and my mother exploding and throwing soup all over the new dining room wallpaper.

"Well, look at that," my father said, cowed into silence.

But the gravel was never weeded, because gardening was beneath a farm laborer's dignity. It was women's work. In those days women had no say; men ruled the world, which was frustrating for my mother as an independent American.

I never knew any of my grandparents, but in these years my mother told me all about her father, an Irish-American lawyer and politician who had first come to Ireland around 1909 with a letter of introduction to a Limerick merchant, the brother of a famous opera singer. Walking up the avenue of the house, my grandfather saw the merchant's daughter riding down it, sidesaddle. That's the woman I'm going to marry, he thought, instantly smitten. He was older than her eldest brother, so my grandmother wasn't so sure of him, but they married and had a son called Donal. For a few years, the family moved back and forth between Ireland, New York, and Santo Domingo in the Dominican Republic where my grandfather had been appointed a diplomat by Woodrow Wilson, for whom he had been a stump speaker.

My mother told other stories: how her parents had returned to Dublin where they founded The Film Company of Ireland, making *Knocknagow*, one of Ireland's first feature films; how my grandfather had been interred during the 1916 Rising and sentenced to death but later reprieved. Two more children, Stephen and Ellen, were born by then, with my mother arriving in 1918. But tragedy struck when the eldest child died of typhoid the next summer. My grandmother caught the fever too. At the time her husband was returning from promoting his films in America, and on arrival at Cobh, he learned that his son was dead and his wife dying. She was buried in Glasnevin Cemetery with her son. My grandfather returned to practicing law in New York, until the Wall Street crash and the famous drive to Florida. I always thought that this trip had given my mother her sense of new beginnings, which she retained all of her life. Eleven at the time, she had left behind her coat, thinking it wouldn't be needed in a hot climate.

Chapter Four

While my mother was having Freddie, my youngest brother, I had my first asthma attack. It must have been something to do with missing her, or wanting to imitate her, or subconsciously craving attention. My father brought me to his old family doctor on the North Circular Road. I was nine and had started developing, so I remember being embarrassed in front of the two men. But the doctor was a cheerful, old-world type who warned me, "Avoid fog, frost, and east wind." I've tried to do so ever since, but it's impossible in Ireland.

The facts of life still puzzled me and I had tried to figure out the sex of horses: which was the *man* horse and which the *woman* horse? They must have different sexes like humans, but how did you know which was which? They all looked the same and I couldn't see any difference underneath.

One day my father was grooming a horse in the big shed.

"Daddy, could that horse have a foal?" I asked.

He continued working and didn't answer. Afterwards he was furious with me for embarrassing him in front of his workman. I was puzzled at the time, but to his generation, sex, even if to do with horses, was a forbidden topic, so it was never discussed. There was no sex instruction from parents or teachers: you were meant to learn everything by osmosis. I thought it was something to do with nature study because of what my mother had told me about God planting a seed in the mother's heart, which grew into a baby.

My father had us praying for purity at a young age. "My strength is as the strength of ten, because my heart is pure," he said. At weekly confession, we were supposed to list "impure thoughts." I had no idea what they were, but confessed anyway. Everyone had them and I didn't want to be different.

There was also hush-hush gossip about Nurse Cadden, a famous backstreet abortionist, who lived near our charlady, Delia, in Dublin's Hume Street. A woman had died during an abortion from a ruptured artery, and

Nurse Cadden had left her body outside on the street. It was a big scandal at the time when everything sexual was considered sinful and sins were always secrets. When I was noticed doing my homework at the kitchen table, the whispering stopped and I was sent out of the room. No one talked in front of children then, and certainly not about sex.

My second school was the Holy Faith, Glasnevin. It wasn't far away but cross-country, and getting there involved taking two buses. Again, if one were missed, there was a long trek home. The uniform was a horrible navy tunic and a navy gabardine coat. The nuns were strict, and an ominous belt hung like a long leather tongue from their waists. They didn't hit us with this, but with a shorter, thicker strap, an educational aid which terrified me. Since I didn't know any Irish and didn't seem able to learn it, I was threatened. I had a phobia about the Irish language, probably because my mother insisted that it was unfair that the repressive Irish State forced children of an American citizen to learn it. Later in life I became a teacher myself, and this block on my part helped me understand how a child can sit in a class and miss out.

At the Holy Faith I came down with one psychosomatic illness after another. I lived in fear, stumbling over my Irish reading. One day I was told if I didn't know my homework by the next day, I would be sent to the office. I'd seen girls crying and holding their hands as they came back to the classroom. Pain and humiliation were awaiting me, but before anything happened, my mother took me out of the school.

"You're not going back there!" she said.

So I stayed at home for the rest of the year, reading books on my own. I suppose I fell behind, but it was liberation to mind Freddie, the new baby, whom my father had welcomed as he had welcomed us all. I remember him hovering over my brother's cot, hanging bath towels on the rails to cut out drafts.

Childhood is a time of waiting—waiting for the holidays, for your birthday, your brother's birthday, for Christmas. Time seems endless, and it was for us as we waited for our parents outside McPhillip's in Drumcondra. For some reason, this pub was one of their favorites, and on the way to or from town, they always stopped there, leaving me in charge of the younger children outside in the car, since my brothers were away in school. Sometimes we got crisps and a Club Orange, but it always ended in fights between my overtired siblings. My mother later told me that she accompanied my father only for his safety. After several hours, he would say, "Let's go back to the children."

In the long Dubber nights, my mother and I often waited in bed for him to return from other pubs. At these times she told me more stories: about her American youth, coming back to Ireland, especially about meeting my father for the first time. She had just left the Mater, and was on a train, returning from Connemara, where she had been on holiday in the summer of 1941. She set the scene dramatically. "It was wartime and I was engaged to someone else."

A stranger came into her carriage. "Is this seat free?"

She had nodded coolly. My father was a shortish young man with a high forehead, thick fair hair, amused brown eyes, and even, white teeth. "He was a Spencer Tracy look-alike," she said. "I was attracted, but played hard to get. Always play hard to get."

Feigned disinterest was the way to attract a man, though this hasn't been my experience. You looked, then looked away quickly. Another tip was to drop a glove when parting from someone you were keen on—then you could ring up to ask if he had found it, and the relationship might go further.

In photos of the time, my mother was slim, with long legs and perfect teeth. Her hair was dark, and she was pale, with electric blue eyes and thick Elizabeth Taylor eyebrows. She was supposed to have resembled the 1930s movie star Deanna Durbin.

"It was my fate," she whispered. "If you believe in fate, it makes life easier."

She stayed regularly with her Irish relations and was taking the train from one set of cousins to another. But despite their kindness, she was lonely because her sister and brother were far away in the United States, to which she returned yearly to keep her citizenship in order. Since she was a natural citizen, this must have had to do with her Irish birth.

I had heard the story again and again.

"I was stuck in Ireland," she sighed. "The war had started and the last boat had left. I didn't take it because I wanted to finish my training."

A photo of the time shows her sitting in a field, wearing a straw hat, dreamily picking daisies—I'm sure it was taken before my father and she met. Was she thinking about an admirer? Her fiancé? He loves me. He loves me not? My father sat down opposite her in the train. "At first we didn't speak," she said.

My mother had had many admirers before my father. The first was a young Mater houseman, Walter Somerville. "He walked me up and down Eccles Street, saying he couldn't afford to get married."

"But he was a doctor," I said in disbelief.

"They earned ten shillings a week!" She sighed. "I should've said I could afford it."

An inheritance had come from her mother, but Walter went to England, later becoming a prominent cardiologist. The next beau was a New York Assistant District Attorney. When my mother refused to return to the States before the war started, he broke it off. "I wept because there was no one to tell," she said, but she must have mended quickly because she soon got engaged to another doctor. "I used to pray my children wouldn't look like him," she giggled. But now Mr. Right had arrived.

"Coming from the west?" my father enquired, as the train left Athlone.

She nodded again, studying the passing countryside.

He took out his cigarettes, packed in a silver case, and offered her one. "Smoke?"

She shook her head.

"Mind if I do?"

"No."

He lit up. Although a man-about-town, whose suits were tailored in London, he was wearing work clothes that day. He was traveling from a cattle fair by train because private motoring was banned during the Emergency. Her coolness only spurred him on, and he finally got her to chat.

"Fancy a drink sometime?" he asked, as they neared Dublin.

My mother refused.

Snubbed, he laughed it off. "You might change your mind."

She looked out of the window, as he finished his cigarette.

My father was popular with women and a favorite bachelor uncle to his nieces and nephews. He was extravagant, so always bought two of everything at once: two suits, two shirts, two pairs of shoes. At one time, he even had two cars and two cameras. He told me my mother wasn't impressed with him that day because his clothes were muddy, but she never said that to me. I think she fell in love at once, mistaking him for a dependable type because, when they disembarked at Kingsbridge Station, she ran up the platform after him. "Wait!" she called out. Like the song "Blue Moon," she needed a love of her own, a dream in her heart. Most of all she needed someone to tell things to. She had allowed others to escape and couldn't let him.

"I've changed my mind about that drink."

"Great!" He took her phone number and promised to ring. Their first date was in the Gresham Hotel. My mother ordered a White Lady and gulped it nervously. "Have another to keep the first lady company," he joked.

Her fate was sealed. And mine. The unwanted engagement ring was returned to the doctor through a mutual friend, and my future parents started walking out together. My mother had just landed a nursing job with the Irish Army but didn't take it, as she had met my father. They were now a couple. How much did they see of each other in those first romantic weeks? My mother said they dined out, went to the cinema, or drove to the seaside. My father still lived in his family home on North Circular Road, with an eccentric sister, while my mother stayed in Fitzwilliam Square, a cousin's home—my mother had many first cousins, all descendants of the Limerick merchant. Anyway, they got engaged on August 15, 1941, the feast of the Assumption and anniversary of her own father's death. My father changed his mind the next day, saying that they hardly knew each other. He had been smitten first, while my mother was the keener one now, but seeing that she was so upset, he gave her back the ring. It might have been wiser to wait.

I suggested this to my mother, but she was adamant.

"I was madly in love. I couldn't wait."

How had things changed so much between them?

"I don't want to get married," I said.

"Nonsense. All girls do!" She sighed. "But don't marry an Irishman."

The Westland Row church where they made their vows to each other had been built in 1832, three years after Catholic Emancipation. Like the more modern Catholic churches from my childhood, it was triumphalist and had been built to impress. The wedding Mass was in Latin, with the priest's back to the congregation. Although daunting to stand at the high altar and promise to love, in sickness and in health, so long as they both did live, each did it willingly. My father was thirty-four, my mother twenty-three.

I imagined the reception where everyone would have been happy that she was settled with a man "possessed of a good fortune" and "in want of a wife." For years we had the wedding photo in the living room: my parents are radiantly attired, their guests around them, and the cousin's children, squat on the floor—my mother had insisted on their presence. We had my father's top hat too, which we used for fancy dress at Halloween, along with my mother's narrow-waisted, cream silk wedding dress. They were two slim young people whom I had never known. My father, in white tie and morning suit, looks confident of the future, while my mother smiles under a Limerick Lace veil, a family heirloom.

The story goes that her nationalist grandfather, when Mayor of Limerick, had refused a civic welcome to the Prince of Wales, the future Edward VII, during his 1885 visit to Ireland, so the lace-makers, who had made gifts for him to bring to his mother, Queen Victoria, were to lose financially, since their work could not now be presented. To compensate them, my great-grandfather had bought it up and had it made into veils. Ever since, women of the family could wear one at their wedding. I was married in a register office, so wore ordinary clothes.

No one thought my father would ever settle down, but his land was entailed, so he had to produce a son—otherwise it went to his brothers' sons—there had been no mention in my paternal grandfather's will of daughters inheriting. It was a Jane Austen plot, although I doubt this was my father's motive for marriage. He wanted children and so did my mother, who belonged somewhere at last. No longer homeless, she prayed at her wedding that any misfortune would come early. "Then I could look forward to my old age," she told me. All her models for marriage—her parents', her cousins', her sister's—had been happy. Why should hers be different?

Because of the war, my parents spent their honeymoon in Kerry. My father, an amateur photographer, took the "selfies" of the day with a timing device, portraying himself as a moody, fashionable, young gent and my mother as a slim, romantic girl. Smoke was in her eyes and she knew her love was true. Everything had looked hopeful, but the cracks in the marriage had appeared early. "Daddy got angry because I brought books on our honeymoon," she told me sadly. "I knew our marriage was a mistake even then." This conclusion always shocked me.

Chapter Five

Between the ages of nine and twelve I attended the Sacred Heart Convent, Mount Anville. Boarding schools were more usual then, and we went because my mother worried about our father's drinking. I had no grudges about going away: I was now as good as my brothers and would be equipped to earn my living one day. Besides, I had read the Chalet School books by Elinor Brent-Dyer, so was looking forward to midnight feasts and dormitory pillow fights.

Since there was no uniform coat, I wore my fitted green tweed with its green velvet collar to school. Mother Alexander, a small, tubby nun with a white biscuit paper around her face, kissed me on arrival with my parents in the entry hall. "Welcome, my dear." This mortified me. I didn't know nuns kissed.

There were two types: Mothers, who wore white cuffs, and Sisters who didn't—one lot taught and the others did the housework. The school building was enormous, and there were around a hundred and fifty girls. In the previous century Queen Victoria had carved her initials on one of the huge cedars in the grounds. The school celebrated its centenary in my first year, and bishops and other eminences came for the festivities. In our white dresses, veils, and gloves, we spent hours in the chapel for the endless ceremonies. Before the whole community, we renewed baptismal vows, renouncing Satan and all his works and pomps.

The many school uniforms were equivalent to a wedding trousseau and had been supplied by Switzer's of Grafton Street, from a list sent with the prospectus: 1 brown weekly tunic; 2 cream summer blouses; 2 brown winter jumpers; 1 brown Sunday dress with 2 white detachable collars; 1 blue gingham Sunday summer frock; 1 white formal dress; white gloves; a black veil; a white veil; 1 divided skirt for games; 2 pairs of Start Rite indoor shoes, with a Mary Jane strap; 1 pair of strong outdoor shoes with laces; 6 pairs of knee socks; 3 vests; 7 pairs of white knicker linings; 3 pairs of heavy brown knickers.

We wore the "linings" under brown bloomers that came to our knees. Every item was marked with my name and number on Cash's tapes, and packed in a school trunk marked MRC 16. I was now a set of initials and a number. I don't remember feeling lonely at Mount Anville: the school cost too much, and I was aware of my parents' sacrifice in sending me. I worked hard, as I wanted to please them.

The strangest thing was to be treated as a child. At home I had been in charge of the others, my mother's Girl Friday. Now the juniors' half-past seven bedtime was a torment because we weren't allowed to read in bed, but I entertained myself by inventing stories, something like *The Secret Garden*. Or else I was an orphan like in *Anne of Green Gables*, with an eccentric aunt and uncle. I invented nightly episodes, with myself as heroine. I also acted out stories from the novel *Black Beauty*, which I shared with a new best friend during daytime recreation.

Although I had landed among strangers, life was a novelty. In my first term, I was picked for the part of a shepherd boy in the nativity play and wore a tea towel around my head. My acting ability was still nil and I had the same stage fright. But there were other extracurricular activities, and the nuns' great sense of occasion. They celebrated feast days by allowing the seniors to raid the dormitories and pull the juniors out of bed for fun. I was intrigued and wondered how girls that big were still at school. What age were they? Surely they were grown-ups. The school seemed a lost kingdom of *Gulliver's Travels*, somewhere between Lilliput and Brobdingnag, a place where children were giants. On their first visit, my parents looked shrunken when I went to the parlor.

"Have you made friends?" my mother asked worriedly.

"Yes . . ." I couldn't think of what else to say. There was a new formality between us, and I was nervous with my own parents.

The next Sunday they brought Lillian, my mother's niece, newly arrived from Florida. She was a small round person, the eldest daughter of Auntie Ellen, and had come to University College Dublin to study for an Arts degree. There had been intense excitement about this because my mother hadn't seen her since she was a child. It's funny how some moments freeze in memory. Lillian was dressed in what I later knew as the Ivy League style, and was full of deep-southern personality. Although I was going on ten, and she eighteen or nineteen, we were the same size. We met in the terraced garden at the side of the main house, where she hugged me. "My Irish cousin!" I was red with embarrassment. But I didn't see her again until Christmas when she came to stay in Dubber.

Before I returned to school after the holidays, my mother warned me that the nuns didn't like people in "trade." I didn't understand this, but obeyed her instruction to say that my father was a "gentleman" farmer. Seniors teased me about this, asking endlessly what my father did for a living.

When I told them again, it caused giggles.

"And where do you live?" they asked.

"North County Dublin."

This gave rise to more giggles.

"Mary Rose sat on a pin," they shrieked. "Mary *Rose*!"

I laughed with them but did not understand the humor. Fear had frozen my brain. There were other small tortures. One was singing class. I was always the one out of tune, so the nun would call me to the piano and play a note, saying, "Sing aah."

I would open my mouth and croak.

"Aah . . . aah," the nun would repeat, hitting the piano again.

My croaking would get worse, until she told me to go back to my place. I was declared tone deaf, and given a complex about music.

At weekly "Notes" the juniors assembled in St. Anne's Hall and were given a card, called a note: *Very Good*, *Good*, *Fair*, or *Indifferent*. If you got a certain number of *Very Goods*, you were awarded a pink ribbon to wear sash-like across your chest; so many bad notes and you lost it. Girls competed to see how many times they could receive and then forfeit a ribbon. It was torture to collect my note, handed out by the Reverend Mother in front of the Junior School, and I got *Indifferent* once, for writing a letter in study. It was a game: by now I had a best friend and we passed the time by writing letters. I pretended that she had broken chairs and desks for which her parents had to pay vast sums of money. A novice found it and told on me. My crime was signing "Love, Reverend Mother." But this trouble passed and at the end of each year I won book prizes, which I again dreaded receiving, this time in front of the whole school: one was Grimms' *Fairy Tales*, which I read and reread.

Although we weren't allowed to run in the corridors, we got a rounded education. I read *Oliver Twist*, and learned how to pull a hanky out of my best friend's pocket. Mademoiselle played games with us and taught us her native tongue. "Frère Jacques, Frère Jacques, dormez-vous, dormez-vous . . ." There was a gym mistress as well as a dancing mistress who taught us the polka. As we embroidered or sewed in class, Mother Alexander read us *The Railway Children* or *The Little Princess*. She was my favorite nun and I her "Rose of Tralee." Thanks to her, I knew all my tables: twelve twelves were a hundred and forty-four. But I still knew no Irish because the lay teacher who taught it always talked about famous artists in class: Jack B. Yeats and people like that, who then meant nothing to me. At other lessons, Mother Alexander told us all about the Communists, who were taking over the world, and how Catholics would be the first to be killed. They had tortured Cardinal Mindszenty for the faith in Hungary, and we might also be one day asked to lay down our lives. To be a martyr was the greatest privilege for a Catholic. Our Lord had died for our sake, and a picture of His bleeding heart was displayed in every classroom.

Daily Mass was in Latin then. It lasted for hours, so I often got weak. The attacks came without warning. Everything dissolved into the color of the priest's vestments, as I found my way out of the chapel, bowing on the way to the Mother General. I may have had low blood sugar, but a doctor was never called. I always got a spoonful of Milk of Magnesia and was then isolated in a room in the infirmary. This was blissful. The food was better than downstairs, and served under covered dishes. I read Victorian novels like *Little Lord Fauntleroy* and solved jigsaw puzzles. Sometimes Mother Alexander called to see me with Holme's *Comprehensive Arithmetic*, and I did pages of problems so as not to fall behind the class. I don't remember my mother being told about these strange illnesses, but parents weren't consulted then.

On one visit my mother thought I was pale, so I asked her to request a sleep-in for me in the morning, as had happened with a delicate classmate. In this way I could miss Mass, which I hated. I was immediately accused of putting her up to it, which I denied, but a canny nun sent me to bed early instead of letting me sleep in. This nun was in the habit of jeering about my bladder problems too, which still tormented me day and night. I managed to hide the bed-wetting, but daytime was torture. I was often sent to the linen room for clean underwear and embarrassing scoldings. Nothing in my life has ever been as bad.

One year there was a flu epidemic, and I was sent home after a gothic nightmare about angels bottling children in a basement. When I returned, my mattress was still wet. It gradually dried out, but then for some reason I was told to swop beds with another girl. I was mortified in case she would notice the dried-out stain, which looked like a map of Ireland crisscrossed with rust marks. I was right: she kicked up a terrible fuss, pointing at the incriminating horsehair mattress. It was "disgusting," a word often used and part of our lingua franca. Mother Alexander was called to adjudicate, and the three of us stood by the iron bed, staring at the stain.

"I'm not sleeping there," the girl said.

The nun peered crossly. "I don't see anything."

"But there's a stain!"

"Nonsense! You're imagining things! Turn the mattress if you're worried!"

The girl finally had to take my bed, and I moved to hers. It was before Vatican II, when a nun's word was law: there was *no* stain and that was that. The next bedtime, Mother Alexander pushed the goodnight holy water font into my curtained cubicle as usual, this time singing, "'twas the truth in her eyes ever dawning / That made me love Mary, the Rose of Tralee."

Although the school was exclusive, the food was terrible. We had to eat everything on our plates, even if a worm had crawled out of a sprout. The stringy overcooked meat was purplish and the mashed potatoes riddled with black lumps—to this day I cannot tolerate mashed potatoes. The only edible food was bread and butter, which we had to cut into bite-sized pieces, a rule which was strictly supervised. The older girls often made "imaginary" ham sandwiches with mustard—the strong taste overwhelming the absent ham. Butter had been rationed in the war, but, although that had been over for years, we were allowed only a small pat at each meal. One day a senior was at the dentist and someone ate her pat. The reedy Mistress of Schools noticed the missing butter, and stood by the refectory table waiting for the culprit to confess. We all looked at each other. I don't remember who ate it, but the nun didn't move until someone owned up. Later she wouldn't allow me to do embroidery on a Sunday, as it was breaking the Sabbath. That was 1950s Ireland.

In my second year, Mary Robinson, our future President, slept in the next cubicle, although we weren't friends because she was in the class above. I made my Confirmation that year in the huge, newly built Mount Merrion church, having learned the catechism by heart. Despite this, I missed a question from the infamous Archbishop McQuaid, who singled me out from the middle of a long row. Not expecting this, my brain turned to wood and I feared being denied the sacrament, but he answered the question for me and my Confirmation went ahead, sponsored by a senior. My parents were in the church and afterwards I went home for the day, and my mother cooked her famous deviled eggs and meatloaf, my favorite foods.

Back in school that night a nun accused me of talking in the dormitory.

"Don't lie!" she scolded, as I hesitated.

"I was," I admitted, feeling the Holy Ghost's presence. I was now a strong and faithful Christian ready for martyrdom. But I didn't get into trouble, as I had told the truth.

Despite the customary ups and downs at Mount Anville, I always came home with a trunkful of lucky dips, prizes won at the school bazaar for my two sisters. Later they told me how exciting it was to see the trunk on the front gravel and how much they had missed me. "It was lonely without you," Olwyn said later. My father's behavior didn't go with marriage and six children. Now I think how unfair it was that they had had to cope with my father's drinking. But I left the school after nearly three years.

Chapter Six

My mother again planned to visit America when my brother Freddie was a baby, but she went instead to stay with Auntie Bronwyn in Belfast. She later told me the story of how, after breakfast in bed one morning, she noticed a framed baby photo of Alistair, Auntie Bronwyn's eldest son, then my age and in boarding school in England. "Amazing how all babies look alike," she said innocently.

Auntie Bronwyn, who had come in to collect the tray, got more and more nervous, as my mother studied the photograph, making complimentary remarks. "Freddie's the image of Alistair at that age. . . . They could be twins, don't you think?"

Her best friend grabbed the photo and hurried from the room. My mother was puzzled, but let it go. It was odd behavior, but so what?

One night my father was out late, so my mother and I hid in the big double bed with the familiar blue floral bedspread and matching bolster, waiting in the dark for his return. Once their marital bed, it was now moved to the back nursery, because my parents had twin beds, deciding they had had enough children. We lay in the dark, telling each other secrets. Then, falling into a funny silence, my mother dabbed on cold cream.

"What's wrong?" I sensed something was upsetting her.

"I can't tell you . . . you're too young."

"I'm not."

"You are." She hesitated, then whispered, "Well . . . remember the head priest . . . from the boys' last school?"

My brothers had now changed schools. "Yes . . ."

"I've . . . he loves me."

He was the jolly man who had walked me up the school steps saying, "One, two, three, four, five, six, seven / All good children go to heaven."

I sat up in bed. "But . . . you're married to Daddy."

"I can't help that!" She shook her head. "I shouldn't have told you. Don't tell anyone!"

"No."

Daddy went mad in drink, but was always sorry afterwards. I couldn't imagine her not loving him. That would be terrible. Would she pack her case and leave again? It was my one dread. What kind of love did she mean? Was it the same as in the films and songs on the radio? Everyone talked about it there, how it could suddenly happen, but what did it feel like?

"Is it like I love Barry?" I asked.

My mother sighed. "When a man and a woman are in love, they're all the world to each other."

I fell asleep, imagining this "all-the-world" love. Whatever it was, I had to get it for her. Everything was Daddy's fault. Being unkind was the worst thing in the world. If he wasn't careful, she would go back to America without us. Then what?

Lillian, our American cousin, always cheered things up. She continued to arrive in Archer's taxis for Dubber Christmases. When she first came, she had worn a fantastic white trench waterproof, which reminded me of Audrey Hepburn's, and in later years I longed for one like it. She had trunks of clothes—someone must really have loved Lillian to buy her such a trousseau, I thought. In our big family, good clothes were few and for Sunday. But by degrees my cousin had evolved into a tiny Marilyn Monroe with peroxide blonde hair, kohl-lined eyes, and outlandish clothes. She seemed to be all circular stripes, which did nothing for her butterball figure. In 1950s Ireland, she was a curiosity, and must have livened up sedate University College Dublin.

A problem with growth hormones accounted for her size. It was feared she would not develop normally, and it was in compensation for this that she had been sent to Ireland. But this was another worry for my already overburdened mother, because my father disliked Lillian. First off, she had made the mistake of asking him to fill her hot water bottle. I never understood what was so terrible about this, but my father came from a generation served by women—he didn't take to American customs where the head of the family did such a lowly thing. Irish young people were seen and not heard. But Lillian wasn't aware of my father's dark side, so there must have been tolerance for her at first. After all, she was my mother's niece and, except for other, more distant relations, alone in Dublin digs.

My two sisters called her "Illian." They in turn were named by her—"Moonfaced Mo" and "Towheaded Mo," which weren't bad descriptions. I had missed out on a nickname by being in boarding school. Like most Americans, Lillian was intensely patriotic. My mother had explained that American school children were brainwashed and had to pledge daily allegiance to the flag before morning lessons. This must have given Lillian a sense of superiority because we had heated arguments about the merits of Ireland versus the United States. According to Lillian, everything there was better than everything in Ireland.

"Bet you don't have Jacob's Cream Crackers!" I finally came up with some tiny superiority. It was well known that Jacobs, the famous Irish bakers, had invented water biscuits.

"Baloney," Lillian said, extolling the virtues of American crackers, of which there were dozens of varieties: Saltines, Graham crackers, Ritz crackers—the list was endless. But I liked her because she was cheerful and treated me as an equal. She came from an exotic world that would one day be mine—the grown-up world of *Seventeen* magazine (which she lent to me), books, and college degrees. One day I would go to college in America and have a trench coat like hers.

My father finally forbade my mother to invite Lillian to the house. His irritation was so strong that she couldn't risk it. So I was sent into town on Sundays during the school holidays to bring her to the pictures. As my mother frantically pressed money into my palm, I was instructed to go for a club sandwich in the Savoy or Metropole café after the film. I dutifully took a bus into the quays and we met under Clerys' clock. Then we went to the matinée and had a meal afterwards. I paid for everything, on strict orders from my mother.

Lillian, dwarfed behind a wedge of sandwich, always asked after my father.

"He's fine," I would lie.

To her he was the charming Irishman her aunt had married. She never had a clue about our father's drinking or his animosity towards her, my mother later learned. Or maybe Lillian was too polite to mention it.

Bernie, our strict nanny, returned while we lived in Dubber. Because I was still away at Mount Anville, I saw little of her at this time, although I have a memory of her killing a chicken for the Sunday lunch. Someone had to do it, and she was a farmer's daughter, so it was not an unusual task for her. But I found it horrible that the chicken ran around the yard headless and that we ate animals. I still resented the physical and mental pain Bernie had inflicted on me, but I had never told anyone. My parents hadn't changed their high opinion of her. She had brought order and structure to our life in the past and now she would do so again. My father was especially pleased that the house would be tidy, but one day he asked my mother, "Have you noticed Bernie?"

She was puzzled. "Noticed what?"

"She's pregnant."

Bernie had been afraid to tell my mother: she had been nervous of telling anyone, particularly her own parents. It would have broken their hearts and finished any chance she had of marriage. Although the man usually got off scot-free, the fate of an unmarried mother then was disgrace and imprisonment in a Magdalene laundry. Before washing machines came in, hotels, restaurants, and the Dublin middle-class sent out their weekly wash in big wicker baskets, and it came back clean and carefully ironed, providing the convent's income. Working in one of these laundries would have been Bernie's fate if my parents hadn't rescued her. I'm glad to say that they were both nonjudgmental and uninfluenced by the narrow-minded society of the time. During her pregnancy Bernie could live incognito with us because Dubber was so isolated, and no one ever came down the lane. After the birth, my mother helped to have the baby adopted privately, so Bernie's parents never knew.

But it was painful for Bernie. Afterwards, she wanted to find her child, but the gynecologist had made all the arrangements, so my mother didn't know where it had gone. My mother deliberately wanted it like this. It was hard, but she was doing her best, according to the customs of the time. At least nowadays unmarried mothers can keep their babies if they choose, although adopted children still have no access to records until they are eighteen. I didn't hear Bernie's story until years later, but the fate of Irish unmarried mothers inspired my first novel, *Mothers*, where three women have the same fate at different times. It was fine to be pregnant in the Ireland of that day, so long as you were married.

Chapter Seven

My best friend had already gone to school in England, so it eased the pain of leaving Mount Anville. After that, Olwyn and I went to a day school in Templeogue. The Christian Education order had arrived in Ireland from England, and my parents were interested in their different methods of teaching. It meant new uniforms and another double bus ride to the south side, so we were permanently exhausted by travel. While waiting for the infrequent Dubber bus, we killed time at Clerys in O'Connell Street. This iconic part of Dublin's history, recently closed down, was a big country shop then. It sold everything from Peggy's Leg, a yellow candy rock-bar, to Wellington boots, and all the clothing seemed to cost 9/11 or 19/11, which is about fifty cents or a eruo in today's money. Burly, red-faced Mr. Guiney stood sentry at the bottom of the stairs, guarding his kingdom, as Olwyn and I lingered over the sweets. It was late when we finally got the bus home, but my mother revived us with Lucozade, then new on the market.

There was a problem meeting the new school's fees so, after a term, we changed to the less expensive Holy Faith in Haddington Road, for which we had to buy yet more new uniforms. I was back with the hated Order, whose nuns wielded the strap. I was no better at Irish, so again I lived in terror. But we were not destined to stay longer than a term in that school, as there were soon to be more serious changes in our family. In Dubber House a mirror had fallen off the drawing room wall and smashed to bits which, to my mother, was an omen and foretold seven years' bad luck. My mother believed in luck and used to say that houses were like people, there were good houses and bad houses. Dubber was a bad house with an unhappy history.

Since my mother couldn't manage the house and six children, Anne came to work for us at this time. A buxom Bessie Bunter, she was a fifteen- or sixteen-year-old orphan from the Sacred Heart Home, a redbrick building which still stands in Drumcondra. I don't know how she ended up with us;

perhaps my mother wanted to help a deprived child, which would have been in her character. Or maybe the wages were less. Anyway, Anne was a plain girl with a cardboard suitcase for her few ugly clothes: baggy skirts and too-tight shrunken jumpers that she burst out of. Her straight brown hair was cut in a pudding bowl style, held off her pudgy face by a childish clip. I saw her neglect and need for love. I was lucky to have a mother.

Anne was still growing, so she was always hungry. She ordered apple tarts on the bill from the breadman without permission and scoffed them in the secrecy of her small bedroom, which was off the kitchen. Everything in those days was bought on tick, which was an agreement to pay later. "Don't tell," she begged me, when I discovered her hiding one under a pillow.

"I won't . . . but Mummy won't mind."

Anne's room was full of crumbs and smelled of a wet bed. I had sympathy with this affliction, which had been mine but by now had cleared up, so we became good friends. I was intrigued by her stories of the orphanage and the cruel nuns with their huge white, elephant-ear headdresses. Anne had been beaten, starved, and locked in cellars, yet she was amazingly cheerful. Instead of working, she spent all her time talking or reading true-love comics which she then lent to me. In return, I swapped my weekly comics: *Girl* and *Schoolfriend.*

"No good," she said, giving them back after a cursory glance.

"What's wrong with them?"

"No love!"

I thumbed through her small, square, illustrated romance, like one of the modern-day graphic novels. It was full of women with big lips and men with square jaws and wasn't my thing either, but I didn't like to say so.

"I'm marryin' a doctor," Anne said. "What about you?"

"I haven't decided yet."

"Do ya have a fella?"

"I'm twelve." Maybe I wouldn't need a husband after all? Because of my father's drinking, I was turning against marriage. "I'm going to be a nurse."

Anne puffed out her fat cheeks. "Maybe a surgeon for you then."

I considered this possibility. I'd seen *Doctor in the House* and had a crush on Dirk Bogarde. Maybe someone like him would be OK for a husband? He didn't look like a drinker.

We talked so much the housework often didn't get done. I always helped Anne, so my mother wouldn't get annoyed, not that she ever would be for long. She was understanding and easygoing and got cross only with my father. Then her rage was impressive.

One day social workers came and took Anne shopping. Her new clothes had that just-bought, new smell, but were for a child, rather than for a young woman: a pleated skirt and a pink, puffed-sleeved blouse. Anne looked at them with scorn and threw them over a hedge. After that, she started staying out late and soon afterwards was sent to a girls' home in Kilmacud. I missed our chats, but I suppose my mother couldn't manage her. These days I pass her Drumcondra orphanage, now a home for the blind, and am reminded of that 1950s class-divided society. I often wonder what kind of life Anne had. The Irish today blame the church or the state for past cruelties to children. We pretend the truth has only now been revealed about the institutions used to warehouse those who didn't fit in. But the horrors of orphanages and reform schools were well known. Although it would never have happened to us, we were threatened with one if we behaved badly. Another threat, this time from my parents, was that we would end up as road sweepers if we didn't work hard in school. They were determined we had to achieve something in life.

I awoke one night to find my mother in bed beside me. I had a déjà vu feeling. My father was cursing downstairs, drunk again and acting irrationally.

"What's wrong with him?" I whispered.

My mother held up the car key. "He wants to go out."

"Gunt!" I heard him shout up the stairs.

I was frightened. What was he saying? It sounded like Irish, but he didn't know any. No one in the family did. My mother hugged me. "Shhh. Don't listen."

There was a loud smash downstairs. Then another. And another.

We had priceless antique china—gold-painted cups, wedding presents from relations, which were kept in the dining room corner cabinet. The set had somehow escaped six children but now my father was smashing it, piece by piece. He was breaking up the house too. Finally the noise stopped. An eerie silence followed. Then the stairs creaked as he stumbled up them. He looked in a few bedrooms, stopping outside mine. Frozen, we held our breath as he tried the handle. It was locked from the inside.

He rattled it again. "I know you're in there!"

I got ready to protect my mother: to kill for her sake. I'd be sent to prison, but I didn't care. I now understood murderers. In the end, nothing happened. He went to bed, falling into a drunken sleep.

The next day I asked my mother what a "gunt" was.

"It's a bad word, darling. Daddy didn't mean it."

"But what does it mean?"

She didn't answer for a minute. "You know the facts of life?"

"It's a womb then?"

"I told you it's a bad word!"

"But womb's not so bad?"

"I want you to forget it!"

I was still puzzled. Later I checked the dictionary, but there was no such word.

My father now usually went to the pub by himself. When he came home, he ranted against everyone: his mother, who hadn't loved him; the Belfast Protestants who had cursed the Pope, causing the Titanic to sink; the Jews who had murdered Jesus and been punished by the Nazis. I had read *The Diary of Anne Frank*, so I got angry. How could he say that? Jesus was a Jew, in case he hadn't noticed. And what about his precious Virgin Mary? She was Jewish, too.

"The Romans murdered Jesus!" I yelled, "And the Titanic hit an iceberg!"

I got slapped across the face but didn't care.

My mother's "love affair" was fading too. The teacher in question had met her for the pictures where they had held hands, she told me secretly. But soon afterwards he broke off the "liaison." I was recruited to write to him and say how mean this was to Mummy. I did this with a Conway Stewart fountain pen, writing scratchily on blue Basildon Bond notepaper, and my mother checked it for mistakes. I couldn't bear to see her unhappy. I suffered if she suffered. It was the same feeling as at my First Communion when I wanted the cheaper dress.

I got a reply, thanking me for my "concern" and assuring me that "nothing improper" had happened between him and my mother. They were friends, and grown-ups needed friends the same as children. He signed off the letter, "With renewed thanks" for writing, which to me was the essence of refinement. In future I would put "with renewed thanks" at the end of my own letters. Today I think how desperate my mother must have been to confide in me like this, but she had no one else. I was probably twelve, definitely no older, but I understood how lonely and unhappy she was. My mother was unconventional and wouldn't have thought that because a person was in a religious order, he couldn't have feelings. In this case the attraction probably came from loneliness on both sides. Also my mother liked books, but had no one to discuss them with, as my father didn't read. And she had that great gift, an ability to feel. So throughout her life, men of all ages fell in love with her. In later years, at family funerals, her younger male cousins used to tell me how much they had admired her gaiety in their youth.

Our last holiday, when we lived in Dubber, had been spent in Rosslare in 1955. We rented a house, across the road from the beach, which belonged to a woman with the interesting name of "Madame Kelly" and which still stands. The sun seemed to shine every day as we played on the beach or went canoeing in the wetlands of Wexford. But that idyllic August ended, and we returned to the usual problems at home. By now I had noticed my father's incompetence and felt that I could run the farm, if only I were allowed to.

The next summer we didn't go anywhere, because things were worsening financially. One afternoon a bailiff arrived at Dubber to take the last few bullocks. I had tried to guard the paddock gate, but was ignored by the men dressed in funny rubbery raincoats. Weeds were growing everywhere by now and the farmyard cat had disappeared. Then one night my father didn't come home with his usual six-pack of Guinness, after the bona fide pubs closed in the small hours. My mother and I waited in my bedroom. Trying to sleep, we lay quiet as mice, hoping to hear the car crunch on the gravel, as it pulled into the yard, and my father stumbling upstairs to bed.

By dawn he still hadn't come home.

The next day we learned that he had been arrested. My mother had told my father to go and talk to his older brother about selling the farm in order to raise capital for his business. Since my uncle was a trustee, my father needed his permission to sell the land. My father was drunk, so he knocked too loudly on his brother's door. When refused admittance, he got angry and knocked again, so his niece attacked him with a mallet, the guards were called, and my father was taken into custody. This was followed by a hospital stay, a court case, and the County Council's huge counter claim for malicious damages, because they had compensated my uncle. My father had wanted only to talk. I now understood why my mother would never allow us to fight.

Except for Freddie's green secondhand trike, I don't remember our last country Christmas. Olwyn later told me that she got a toy lawnmower that year, and Evie a toy vacuum cleaner, so funds must have been low. Although five in all, the Dubber Christmases have blurred together. If I remember one, it's because of some event, like the time Barry nearly died again. He got acute appendicitis in the middle of Christmas dinner and was rushed to Temple Street Hospital, wrapped in a blanket, to be operated on by the head surgeon, a relative by marriage, who had abandoned his turkey dinner to stand in for a tipsy registrar. All was well in the end, but was it another omen? My mother thought so. A neighbor also believed that Dubber House was unlucky and advised my father to take his six children by the hand and walk down the lane. Next thing the farm was to be sold at auction. "What should I do?" my father asked my mother, as the auctioneer held the hammer in mid-air. "Let it go," she whispered. "Let it all go to the bottom of the sea."

That was my mother's philosophy, but the farm did go for a song. A vet had bought it and immediately resold the house and paddocks, which were free of entail, on to my cousin, another trustee of my father's estate. He was getting married and wanted to live in the house because it bordered on his own father's farm. When my father later regretted his mistake, the vet agreed to rescind the sale, but this relative would not agree to return Dubber House. So that New Year we heard the Christ Church bells from the front gravel for the last time. We had lost our Eden and my father was crying, as we drove across the city to Dún Laoghaire, leaving everything behind. "You'll weep like this one day," he said, seeing my shocked face.

Chapter Eight

But our luck hadn't run out completely. Dún Laoghaire had been chosen as the ideal place to live when my mother was having a hysterectomy in St. Michael's Hospital there. Thanks to Sister Veronica, my mother's friend from Mater Hospital days who was now the hospital's matron, my father had gone there for a rest after his terrible row with his brother. When he recovered, my parents had gone house hunting. As well as the two Dún Laoghaire piers, the sea air, and the yachts in the harbor, there were trains and buses to Dublin, and good local schools.

I was turning thirteen when we moved, and my mother returned to nursing for the first time since her marriage. I loved the new house. Now we wouldn't need holidays because we lived by the sea and were on permanent holiday. Number 4 Myrtle Avenue, which is still there, was a double-fronted 1950s style semi-detached at the end of a row of four. The farmhouse had been bigger, so perhaps that's why the new house seemed so small. Or maybe it was our family of eight. It had single-glazed windows, making the house cold, and a high-pitched roof. Glass bricks were in the porch and it stood on a corner at right angles to seedier Royal Terrace. The railed-in field opposite was for hockey in those days. A gothic orphanage backed onto the far end, making a square.

I hated my mother going off every night—other mothers didn't and I missed her so much, but she depended on me, so I could not complain. Money was a necessity, but it was now tight because, although we had sold the land, we had not yet been paid. But, despite my objections, my mother loved working and was proud of having a profession. Women were second-class citizens, she told me, especially in Ireland. If she were run over, my father could sue the motorist for damage to his property: a husband owned his wife. Despite this, she believed women to be the stronger sex, which was why I had been her confidante from a young age.

The new house was rented for three hundred pounds a year. We arrived with a live-in maid, so we must have had some money, but I don't remember her clearly or how long she stayed. My parents had the master bedroom, but still kept to separate beds. The younger children shared, while I had my own room, and my two brothers were mostly away at school. Although she didn't believe it as an American, my mother often quoted the thinking of the time: girls got married, so I would too. I wouldn't have to support a family. It would be different for my brothers: they had to be breadwinners, so they needed a stress-free childhood. Still, I was fussed over too: because of my asthma, I had my own room with a rubber mattress and pillows to prevent allergies. I often got a hot toddy for a cold, which my father believed cured all ills. I discovered early on that any of their children's illnesses united my parents. My aim was still to keep them together, no matter what.

The landlord, a Plymouth Brethren member, lived around the corner, but we hardly ever saw him. We did know the Fergusons, the white-haired Church of Ireland couple next door. They were good neighbors and never complained about our untidy garden, although it must have irked them. They had me in for tea regularly, and lent me out-of-print books on the British Royal family, with pictures of the two princesses in Girl Guide uniforms. Is that where I got my obsession? I yearned to be a Girl Guide, sleep in a tent, and learn about knots and how to start a fire by rubbing two twigs together. I had even studied Morse code. But there weren't any Catholic Guides then, at least not locally, and, although my mother promised we could join the Church of Ireland, we never did. Recently I found a calendar in an old diary with two weeks crossed out, and "Guides" scrawled across the page—as if I *had* been camping. But no one in the family had ever slept in a tent.

Dr. Paul Singer, of the famous Shanahan Stamp Ponzi scheme, lived three doors down, and his children played with my sisters. He was a burly Bratislavian Doctor of Philosophy, who had duped the foolish Irish into investing in stamps meant to treble in value overnight. The scam collapsed when a robbery took place at the company's office on the eve of a major auction. It prefigured the delusional property bubble of recent times, although the money lost does not compare. 1950s Ireland was in permanent recession, except no one knew it. No one had a bob, few enough had jobs, everything was gray, but this was just the way things were. All photographs were black and white, so when Kodak color came in, it looked false to me. The real world was monochrome.

Our whole family got flu the first freezing winter in Myrtle Avenue.

"Bernie is coming to look after us," my mother announced.

I was in my dressing gown, feeling sick after eating a Cadbury's Turkish Delight chocolate bar. It seems amazing to remember that detail, but I do. "Can't we get someone else?"

My mother looked at me in disbelief. "I thought you all loved Bernie."

I said nothing. Bernie must've been in her late twenties by then because she had first come to work for us as a teenager. The others were delighted of course, but my memory was elephantine, my mother always said. That winter Bernie took command in her usual efficient way. She made us hot drinks and persuaded us to eat her prepared meals, as we lounged around in dressing gowns. We had a television by then and, as we got better, used to undress for bed at the fire under the benevolent gaze of the BBC newsreader, Kenneth Kendall, before the mad dash upstairs to bed and hot water bottles. I was getting on well with Bernie, so I thought that perhaps she regretted her harsh treatment of me, but one night she inquired casually in front of the others, "Do you still wet your knickers?"

I had stopped leaking, but was too shocked to answer. I was five again, red with shame. She had said "knickers," a word I still can't say.

About fifteen years ago, Olwyn and I, driving in County Wicklow, found ourselves near the 1950s home of Bernie's parents, where the younger children of the family had spent holidays. Bernie had always been good about bailing out my mother by looking after them in difficult times.

We stopped beside a ruined cottage.

"I'm sure that's the house," my sister said.

It was. On inquiring, we were told that Bernie now lived down the road in a new bungalow. We found it, but I didn't want to call in, although Olwyn did. My sister is four years younger than me and, as the eldest of the second half of the family, she had obviously missed out on Bernie's cruelty. There are some things you can write about but never discuss: you can tell the whole world, but not your dearest friend. Although then past middle-age, I still couldn't tell anyone about Bernie. Children of the same family have different experiences and different stories to tell, because memory is individual and each child is affected by their place in the family and their particular relationship with their parents and other adults. Bernie must have mellowed in later years and been kinder to my younger siblings because they felt so differently about her.

"She came when we moved to Dún Laoghaire," Olwyn said. "Remember we all had the flu?"

I did remember, but hesitated. "It might be painful for her to meet us."

But it would have been too painful for *me* to meet *her.* I should have agreed to call in, but Freud says that we don't want to be cured of our hurts.

Bernie's modern bungalow had swings in the driveway, suggesting grandchildren. Despite everything, I was glad about that and hoped she had found her lost child. It took me years to understand that Bernie was probably acting out hurts that had happened to her. Did her punishments happen once, or many times? They seemed to go on for a long time, but it is hard to know with memories. Lately I asked Barry his impression of Bernie. "Too strict," he said immediately. "Those round glasses reminded me of the Nazis. But remember, she was very young."

"Why did she hate me?"

"Because you were the favorite."

"I thought it was Maurice."

"He was Mummy's. You were Daddy's."

It still didn't make sense.

My mother never worried about material things, but she was upset when, in the first months in Dún Laoghaire, my father, in another drunken fit, broke her remaining china. "A street angel and house devil," she sighed. He had attacked his brother, and now he was smashing the last of her wedding gifts. This time she didn't clear up the mess, but left the broken bits for him to see the next morning. The dining room was a bomb site as, still in his dressing gown, he stared uncomprehendingly at the debris. His handsome face was pale with red mince-meat blotches, and there were tears in his eyes. "What on earth happened here?"

"*You* did it!" I said.

He shook his head.

"You did!"

He didn't reply. Could he have forgotten?

"You're meant to be our father, not a vandal! You spoil everything!" I was shaking, but ignored my fear. "Only a cuckoo soils its own nest!" My mother always said this in anger.

He looked at me in a curious way, saying nothing. Then he went into the kitchen, ran a glass of water and, trembling, took some aspirin. Shakily, he put on the kettle for a cup of tea. He looked terrible, and all my anger leached away. What was happening to him? We didn't know it then, but a piece of tissue was growing in the wrong place, and this was causing the havoc in our lives.

My father was sent to St. John of God's Hospital in Stillorgan, where a brain lesion was diagnosed for the first time. Whether this had caused his behavior all along, we didn't know. It certainly couldn't have helped him. There didn't seem to be any treatment or even much sympathy or counseling on what he might expect in the future. Everything was matter-of-fact. A brain lesion: but what did that mean? We didn't know, so we shelved it because we couldn't do anything about it. Life became peaceful for a while because my father stayed in hospital, attending AA meetings, making baskets, and painting landscapes of Spanish villages with white sunlit houses and strong dark shadows. As far as I knew, he had never been to those postcard places. I decided he had gone into the wrong business. He wasn't a farmer or a cattle dealer. He took wonderful photographs, as well as painting pictures, and should have been an artist, or got some job where everything was orderly.

My father was forbidden to drink again, but he did, as soon as he got out of hospital—to relieve the pain of life, my mother said. She also said it was better to have a short memory, and not to look back. If you did you could be turned into a pillar of salt like Lot's wife. But my father insisted on remaining homesick for our comfortable farmhouse with its thick walls and cozy Aga; also he missed the trees and fields. And we missed our dogs most of all. We had none in Dún Laoghaire, so we must have found them homes before moving. They weren't suburbanites and wouldn't have known what a dog lead was. My father's regret was twofold: as well as going for a pittance, the farm wasn't totally his to dispose of. It had been entailed to my brother Maurice, but the trustees had allowed it to be sold, instead of looking after his interests. It's all another life now, but it had consequences at the time.

Land and its loss is a theme in Irish literature. It became our family's too, and there was no way back. Once wealthy, we were now poor, as the funds from the sale were held in trust for my father to split with Maurice when he became twenty-one. We depended on the yearly rent from Violet Hill, a field belonging to my father beside Glasnevin Cemetery, and my mother's salary as an agency nurse. For the next seven years, we were milked by lawyers, and Maurice became a ward of court. Although the trustees had promised that my father could recapitalize his meat-exporting business with his share of the sale, it made no difference financially. Brokenhearted, he blamed everyone but himself, especially my mother, who believed Dubber had ruined his life.

Although we had lost the land, we had Dún Laoghaire. George's Street bustled on a Saturday, full of color and activity. When I went shopping with my mother, we queued in the Monument Creamery for fresh eggs, slabs of unsalted butter, and homemade oatcakes. You could window-shop at the two department stores: Lee's and McCullagh's. Both displayed curtains and household goods, along with embarrassing women's corsets. A newfangled supermarket had opened on the corner of Patrick Street, where we bought Shredded Wheat for the first time, which reminded me of hay. There were comics and American magazines in Dixon's Newsagents. I loved comics, as well as books, and spent most of my time reading.

My mother always walked my two sisters to the national school at St. Joseph's Orphanage, around the corner from our house. There they had noticed that the nuns discouraged friendship with the orphans, who also attended the school. This was another class divide of the time: although broke we remained on the right side of it because we had parents. No matter what, they would stick up for us.

I went to the Sacred Heart in Monkstown and got a new gray uniform, a smart gray blazer with red trim, and a beret with a red badge. I had to make new friends, which was a problem for our family did not invite people back to tea, the custom with school friends then. But it was consoling to be a child of the Sacred Heart again. The privilege endowed rights on me. As a past pupil, I could visit any of their convents worldwide, and be sure of a welcome. I imagined this future of travel. Maybe I wouldn't be going to the Alps, but there were other places to visit.

Miss Fortune looked cross as I came into the Monkstown classroom on the first morning. "Why're you late?"

Our family was always late but, feeling all eyes on me, I mumbled some excuse about not knowing the way to the school. Miss Fortune taught English and history and was strict. I pondered on her name, but there was nothing "misfortunate" about her. She was small and blonde, probably not much older than us, and wore an academic gown, which gave her an air of authority and impressed me greatly. As I found my way to a free seat at the back of the class, she held up a copy of the *Reader's Digest*. "It Pays to Increase your Word Power," she said, looking right at me.

I sat down, red in the face.

She wrote words on the blackboard and went around the class, asking what they meant, until she came to "unrequited."

"Anyone know what that means?"

No one answered. I hoped she wouldn't ask me.

"Something which isn't repaid," she said. "Unrequited love, for example, is love which isn't returned."

I should've known, since it had been my mother's problem.

Miss Fortune was one of those memorable teachers, probably the most inspiring I've ever had, because she introduced me to Shakespeare, for which I will always be grateful. A great teacher imparts enthusiasm to his or her students. At thirteen, I was riveted by the language and story of *A Midsummer Night's Dream*. It set my brain on fire.

> *And, as imagination bodies forth*
> *The forms of things unknown, the poet's pen*
> *Turns them to shapes, and gives to airy nothing*
> *A local habitation and a name.*

I would be a writer one day, and give shape to airy nothing. We read *The Merchant of Venice* the following year, and I imagined the pound of flesh hacked from Antonio's body, as I memorized Portia's speech about the quality of mercy.

We had Miss Fortune for history too, studying feudalism and chivalry, the world of knights and their ladies, troubadours and the Children's Crusade. In the late eleventh century, they had marched all the way to the Holy Land to fight the infidel and restore Jerusalem to the true faith—which we were lucky to be in. God had chosen us, so we were sure of Heaven, while pagans rotted in Limbo, or worse, Hell. My first year in that school was happy, and I made friends with a girl called Janet, who lived in Blackrock and never expected to be asked back for tea. Later I got a bike and cycled to school daily, free-wheeling down Monkstown Hill, past the Christian Brothers College, at breakneck speed. It took a quarter of an hour from our house.

Meanwhile my father was in and out of hospital. He was definitely in the wrong job, I decided. Instead of being a meat exporter, he needed something easier. An ideal job for him would've been in the local laundry, where brown paper parcels were stacked neatly on shelves. You handed your ticket in, and the assistant found your laundry. It was methodical and straightforward, but there was no hope of his applying for something so menial.

Although educated in Clongowes, my father wasn't academic. On leaving school, he had wanted to join the Jesuits or the Indian Civil Service, but had to go into the family cattle business. He was devoted to the saintly Father John Sullivan, who had taught him, so we had often visited that priest's grave in the grounds of Clongowes. My brothers had changed to that school, as the Jesuits had agreed to wait for the fees because our money was tied up. The school was a gray forbidding castle with a long avenue. It was full of bully-ing boys and beatings, so I pitied my brothers. On Sunday visits my mother wore her green suit and ermine stole, while my father's fedora was pulled over his eyes like Humphrey Bogart's. A Jesuit dressed in swishing black robes came with us to the graveyard, and jokingly called me "a true Clon-gownian"—I don't know why. He told us stories about James Joyce, who had been a pupil in the school. Later he sent me a book on sex education, *Growing Up, A Book for Girls*, which didn't explain a thing, except "A life-producing fluid passes from the man to the woman." It must mean French kissing, I thought. How else could fluid pass from a man to a woman? It was another riddle, which caused me to stare in horror as boys and girls kissed in the pictures. How could they be so irresponsible? No wonder there were so many unwanted babies in the world.

Around then my mother found out that Alistair, Auntie Bronwyn's son, was my father's love child. As he was about my age, he must have been conceived in the first years of her marriage. There was a terrible row, and angry letters flew back and forth between the two women. My mother packed her case again, but once more my father found the hotel where she had checked in and brought her home.

"If you need a friend, I'll be around," Auntie Bronwyn wrote to my mother.

"I did need a friend and you were around!" my mother replied, adding a postscript that her husband had never loved Auntie Bronwyn, "a chinny bitch" who had thrown herself at him. This was the start of my mother's "snorters," unkind letters telling people what she thought of them. She'd get into a rage and dash one off, without considering the consequences.

Auntie Bronwyn moved out of our lives from then on. My last memory of Alistair is waving goodbye to him at Amiens Street Station, as he ran for the Belfast train with his mother—we were both around twelve. It was a few months before the row, and the two families had met for afternoon tea in the Royal Hibernian Hotel. Alistair was a lanky, dreamy boy, with floppy hair like Freddie's, which is odd because my brother is supposed to resemble my mother. The tea was an effort to keep up appearances, but some tension broke through. After the tea, Auntie Bronwyn's husband had unexpectedly warned my father to "stay away from my children." According to my mother, this could mean only one thing: it was true about Alistair. But the man had bad health and died soon afterwards. My father attended the funeral in a northern monastery, uninvited, where he saw Alistair and his two younger brothers, all in gray flannel school suits, walking behind their father's coffin.

Chapter Nine

With my father in hospital, life was peaceful and I had my mother to myself at last. We went shopping, had cups of tea in Fuller's Café, and even went to the pictures. At the time I was hooked on romantic stories and had discovered Frances Parkinson Keyes' novels. Her characters lived on the southeast coast of America and sat on moonlit decks with escorts in evening dress, sipping mint juleps. They represented my mother's lost life. The life she would have had if she hadn't shared a railway carriage with a handsome stranger on that fateful summer's day. "Never marry an Irishman," she still told me repeatedly. He would only blame me for not having more money. Money was the ugly thing you needed for a happy life.

Although we had none, we could now see more of our cousin Lillian, who was still studying in Dublin. She caught the bus out to Dún Laoghaire to see us. "Don't you miss Dubber?" she asked me once, when I met her at the stop in George's Street. I couldn't say that that world had fallen apart, that Dubber had become overgrown with weeds, and that the workman had left because we couldn't afford his wages. The cats had disappeared too, and rats had multiplied and were running up the drive. No one had ever crossed our threshold. Years later when I read about the Brontë sisters, I thought that we were like them: isolated. The truth was my father didn't like *any* visitors; it wasn't just Lillian. I knew that she thought we had come down in the world, but remember her politely admiring the Myrtle Avenue house, as we walked up Royal Terrace. It was great to have a cousin, and our friendship was to be renewed in my late teens when she always came back for the Dublin Theatre Festival and took me to plays: *The Field* by John B. Keane and *Galileo* by Bertolt Brecht. It was a real treat then, because I hadn't a penny.

While my father was getting treatment, his light blue Volkswagen "Beetle" stood unused in the garage, so my mother started driving it. I won't say she learned, because in those days there were no L-Plates, tests, or lessons—

you just bought a license for a pound and took off. On the whole, women didn't drive then—Aunt Noreen did, but she was different, an independent widow. In the past my father had always driven. When my mother had asked to be taught in Dubber, where she was isolated, he would mutter against "women" drivers, as if it were a man-only skill, although he had allowed me to steer his Chevrolet a few times. Barry, then twelve, had no such gender-based bias. He was into cars, like most boys, and taught my mother from a library instruction book. She took to the roads with relish, drove us to school, visited my father in hospital, and thought nothing of delivering my brothers all the way back to boarding school in County Kildare. Fewer cars were on the roads then, but it was still nerve-racking, especially if she had to reverse. She had not yet mastered this art.

On one occasion, my mother was buying me a dress in Dorset Street for a party at Aunt Noreen's to celebrate her daughter's birthday. It was pre–traffic lights and cars drove higgledy-piggledy across O'Connell Bridge. A young guard, on duty at the intersection of O'Connell and Abbey Streets, halted the traffic imperiously with a white baton. Our Volkswagen was first in line, waiting for his signal to go on. We were surrounded by cyclists, and the pavements on either side of us were crowded with shoppers. Behind us cars lined up like chariots. The world seemed as gray as the General Post Office on our left and Nelson's Pillar ahead; the only color came from my mother's green suit, with its knife-pleated skirt, and her luxurious ermine stole. Her makeup was Max Factor Pan Stick and her lipstick pillar-box red. She was about thirty-nine then, and still beautiful.

The guard directed us to back up, but my mother ground the gears, jolting us forward. He waved his baton furiously. "Go back! Go back!"

She braked and the car stalled. We were stuck mid-intersection. My mother breathed heavily. "What's wrong with the idiot?"

As the guard waved his arms like an orchestral conductor, my heart pounded. "You're to go back!"

"But we're going forwards!"

"There's a white line. You were meant to stop behind it."

She studied the gears. "I didn't see any line."

My mother's philosophy of never looking back was going too far. "We're blocking the way."

The gears ground, as she tried to reverse. The car stalled again and I prayed silently: "Oh, angel of God, my guardian dear, to whom God's love commits me here . . ." Ahead, Nelson watched from his pillar, and I remembered that my mother had seen a man jump from the top of it. I now understood why: life sometimes got too much and this was such an occasion.

"Is it necessary to breathe like that?" she asked.

"I can't help it."

She turned the key and the engine coughed but wouldn't restart. The guard strode over, while overcoated and headscarfed pedestrians stared curiously from the pavement as he towered over the small car. "You've come too far! Now go back, Ma'am!"

My mother looked helpless. "I'm sorry."

He swung one arm underhand, again directing her back. "That's all right. Just reverse now!"

She was about to cry. "I can't!"

He reddened, then, leaning into the open window, explained where the reverse gear was.

She tried again. "It seems stuck."

He glanced impatiently at the traffic backup. "Well . . . let me try."

She got out and the guard sat in the driving seat. I was aware of his handsome looks, as he effortlessly found reverse gear. Checking the rearview mirror, he backed up into the space vacated by the car behind us. Then he got out, returning the key to my mother. I expected her to be charged with dangerous driving. Surely you should be able to reverse before driving down Dublin's main street.

"Thank you," my mother said, getting in. "You're a nice young man."

He cleared his throat awkwardly. "The gears, eh—seem OK . . . but get them checked now."

My mother flashed a white smile and he went back to his perch, furiously directing the cars on from Abbey Street. We awaited our turn, then moved forward in a series of shuddering jerks on up O'Connell Street through Parnell Square and, turning into Dorset Street, managed to park outside the small draper's shop where we got my party dress. It was blue corduroy.

The Volkswagen was sold soon afterwards, and my mother never drove again. Today I'm in awe of her courage. Driving was another dive in the deep end, another immersion in life. She had never hung around the shore, shivering. I was always afraid to drive and spent a fortune on lessons, not passing the test until I was in my mid-sixties. Today I hear her voice in my ear, "Look ahead, not back."

Chapter Ten

With six in the family, we were often short of clothes, but our American aunt always sent a Christmas parcel. It came by regular post, or Lillian or a friend would be persuaded to bring it along with their luggage, sailing across the Atlantic in the days before air travel. Many families at the time received parcels. One year ours was exceptionally big. We all gathered round, waiting expectantly for a present from among the usual motley collection of hand-me-downs, penny loafers, bobby socks, Caribbean straw hats, sunglasses, and other Floridian flotsam and jetsam. Would Auntie Ellen have at last sent anything suitable for the cooler climes of south County Dublin? We had no need for sun hats in wet Irish summers. Even if it were warm enough, we would look ridiculous.

"This isn't bad," my mother said as she pulled a flimsy, shocking-pink strapless dress from the parcel and handed it to me. "It'll fit you."

I was younger than my first cousins, and their clothes either swam on me or were too narrow-waisted. I held this to my front, but it was too big.

"It'll be useful in a few years," she said. "We can get it altered."

I nodded, examining the exotic dress. Even if it were taken in, I would have no occasion to wear it. I had no boyfriend and neither did anyone in my class. Yet the dress would not go to waste. It would hang behind my bedroom door and transport me to other worlds—of boyfriends calling for me in open-top convertibles, of drives along wide roads to the moonlit beach. I would imagine meeting a James Dean look-alike and afterwards we'd sip Coke on the porch, while cicadas buzzed in the hot night air. I'd be popular and beautiful.

There were shirts and funny check trousers for my brothers, but they were both too conventional to wear them. The next gift was a bottle of aftershave. My mother handed this to my father, who sniffed it skeptically. Despite all his problems, a plebeian perfume was not for him.

My mother pulled a can of peanuts from the rubble of clothes. "This gives me an idea."

As usual, my father looked dubious.

"Why don't we import peanuts?"

My mother was always getting ideas to make our fortunes because we constantly needed money. She had thought of marketing potato crisps, new in Ireland then, but had lacked the capital. Peanuts were another popular snack from her youth.

"They're for monkeys!" my father said, who had bought them at the zoo. "You won't get the Irish to eat them!"

"They already do at Halloween," I said.

"These will be roasted and salted," my mother went on.

It was a good idea—roasted peanuts with their millions of fattening calories were not yet on offer in 1950s Ireland. But, like her other brainwaves, it was scooped by someone else. We ate the peanuts that day and that was the end of it. We were destined to remain poor and now lived hand to mouth, getting groceries on weekly tick. We had to pay with our mother's check, which wasn't always on time. As a night nurse, she was often hired by people who couldn't afford the fee. But she wasn't materialistic and never pestered them to pay for their sick relations. "The week rolls around too quickly," she used to say.

I suppose she had an impractical streak. Other mothers weren't like that and didn't think that life would be an adventure. "Think of all the people who could've been born instead of you," she often said. "You were the lucky one. You got there first. You have to use your life." Other mothers didn't sing "Blue Moon" or "The Way you Look Tonight." They hadn't been brought up in exotic Florida where you went to the beach instead of school. They hadn't had love affairs on Atlantic liners before the war. They weren't beautiful, and didn't use Pond's cold cream or *Ma Griffe* perfume. No, they were sensible and recited the rosary and made novenas. They forced their children to do housework, while our mother said, "Leave it, you'll be doing it for the rest of your life." It was great psychology, because we didn't resent doing it then. My mother had to sleep in the day, in order to stay awake at night.

Instead of my mother visiting her sister in America, there was now talk of the whole family emigrating there. It was exciting to think of starting a new life in Florida. My mother had even called to the U.S. Embassy to enquire about visas, but in the end it came to nothing: Auntie Ellen wasn't agreeable to the plan. And we couldn't leave the country anyway because funds were still frozen.

Losing Dubber became an obsessive topic of conversation in our family. Life was divided into before and after. The farm, in the middle of bleak fields, had become rural bliss compared to our more ordinary life of Dún Laoghaire—which I much preferred. My mother did too, but spent her days, when she was meant to be sleeping, going to a solicitor with my father to see about getting back the farm. But, according to her, the solicitor was a venal man who had poisoned her husband's mind against her and given him false hope.

While they were gone, I looked after the younger children. One day the doorbell rang, freezing us to stone. Usually only creditors called: someone to repossess the TV or demand money for some or other unpaid bill, so we didn't open the door when alone. Who could this be?

The bell shrieked again—followed by a loud knocking. Whoever it was wouldn't go away. I peeped out from behind the dining room window curtain. Three girls in the Monkstown uniform of gray coats and berets were at the hall door. My classmates.

"We know you're in there!" one yelled.

I hid behind the curtains.

"We've come for tea." Another shrieked, giggling. "You invited us."

Although desperately wanting friends, I had never yet invited anyone home for tea. Now that we had no help, the house was never tidy. And all the cups were broken, so we had to drink tea out of jam jars. It seems amazing to have been so poor, but we were.

"We know you're in there!" the girls yelled together.

I opened the door an inch, pretending to read my *Girl* comic.

"Hi." I grinned stupidly at the tall busty schoolgirl, bulging out of her coat. Her round face was freckled, and crinkly curls poked from under her beret. Slitty eyes disappeared into the creases of a fat smile. I hated her.

"Hi!" She mimicked a fake American accent.

I don't why she did that because I didn't have an accent. None of us did, although we were still considered Americans.

"We've come for tea!"

I kept my foot in the door. "Sorry, it doesn't suit."

"You invited us."

"Ah, go on, let us in!" The smallest girl had an apple-red complexion. Her coat was too big, and a beret was plonked plate-like on top of two jug-handle pigtails on either side of her head. The third girl, a neighbor and the ringleader, didn't say a word but hovered ominously in the background. I faked calmness, but my heart was hammering, and the words of my comic blurred into each other. My foot still held the door, so it couldn't open. They got friendlier, so I relaxed—a mistake. One of them pushed past me and ran up the stairs. The other two followed, shrieking wildly, as they ran from room to room.

"They don't make the beds!" they chanted, galloping downstairs again. It was like a cowboy film where the Sioux surround the pioneer wagons. I tried to bar their way to the kitchen where the table was still cluttered from breakfast—porridge plates and the jam jars half-filled with tea were witness to our poverty.

"They live like pigs! They live like pigs!" all three screamed, charging downstairs and out of the house, one after the other.

My mother returned to find me in shock.

"I'm not going back to that school."

She took me in her arms. "Darling, you can't run away."

"Yes I can."

"Bullies are cowards. You have to remember who you are."

Her own father had said this to her in difficult times. He had been a poor Irish immigrant who had graduated from Yale University, summa cum laude. His film company had always inspired me, as had his imprisonment in Kilmainham. He had done things with his life. *He* knew who he was. But who was *I*? I hadn't a clue. Anyway, my mother went right down to the school to complain about the girls' intrusion.

The Reverend Mother was sympathetic but insisted that I return the next day. I did, and the culprits were made to apologize. We stood in a circle, and I shook hands with each in turn, although I hadn't forgiven them and never would. I expected a *Tom Brown's Schooldays* vendetta and my life to be a misery for snitching, but there was nothing like that. Everything wasn't the same as in books, and I did finally make friends in that school. Another classmate invited me to a party, but I left the Sacred Heart soon after that.

Chapter Eleven

My mother always made pound cake to cheer us up on wet days. In the early winter of 1959, she broke some news while stirring fudge. "Aunt Noreen wants to send you to boarding school."

I was fifteen and alarmed. "I'm OK in Monkstown."

"You can't turn down an opportunity." She didn't look up from the delicious concoction of cocoa, sugar, and butter. Aunt Noreen had always liked me, she explained. It had started when I was a skinny baby and she'd accused my mother of not feeding me. Now that there was no money in the family, I had to be educated and make my way in the world. The choice was Loreto Abbey, Rathfarnham.

I wasn't impressed.

"Aunt Noreen wants Niamh to have a sister," my mother said.

Niamh already attended Rathfarnham, and Aunt Noreen had gone herself, with her own sisters, decades before. To say someone has a moral compass is a cliché, but clichés say something true. She was a really good person and one of the only relations we knew. Her interest in us was because of the past. My mother often told me the story of how Noreen, the same age as the century, had visited my grandparents when they came back to Ireland from Santo Domingo around 1914. Since they had sailed regularly between the two continents, I imagined that they could have been on the Titanic, except it was going the wrong way. On arrival, they had set up house in Pembroke Road, Dublin, and, during the Rising, Noreen's family had gone there for safety. My maternal grandmother was known for her hospitality—her own family's coat of arms was a pelican, which bleeds its breast for its young. When Donal, her seven-year-old, got sick, it was thought to be from eating clay. He got worse, and my grandmother was told not to nurse him because he was dying: her other children couldn't grow up motherless. When her Jesuit brother told the little boy he was going to heaven, he wasn't too happy about the news, so his mother had promised to go with him. After his death, she went to her father's house in Limerick and immediately fell ill: her last meal was a boiled egg. After she died, her husband and surviving children went back to America. When my mother returned to Ireland in the 1930s, she at first stayed with Noreen's parents. So when things went wrong for us, this relative naturally wanted the best, but it was often unpalatable—like cod liver oil, or boarding schools. My two brothers had by now changed schools and were paid for by another relation. I was to join Niamh when she returned to school after an illness.

"But I have two sisters here," I reminded my mother. They had demolished the fudge, and were now in bed. I didn't want to leave them.

"Niamh has no sister."

"She has a brother," I argued, although he was years older.

"A brother's not the same," my mother insisted. "It's terrible to have no sister."

That was true, but could you order a sister like a gift from a catalogue? We were different people, with different tastes. I liked poetry, while Niamh was scientific, and into hockey and tennis. What if we didn't get on? It was enough to go to tennis hops with her in the summer holidays when I visited. That was "rock around the clock, till the broad daylight." On those occasions, I suffered agonies. I was no good at dancing, and once stood by the wall all evening, until a one-armed boy took pity and asked me up. I have never been so grateful to anyone. It wasn't that I was particularly ugly: I just didn't know anyone.

"Aunt Noreen wants to meet you in town tomorrow," my mother said finally. "You'll need pajamas and things."

I couldn't sleep that night, thinking about the new school. Why couldn't I go back to Mount Anville or stay on in Monkstown? I liked cycling up and down the hill, and had made friends. Now I would have to play hockey and sleep in a dormitory. Besides, my mother needed me. She had no one else to help her.

There's a definite point at which everyone's childhood ends—going to Rathfarnham was mine. I didn't want to leave home, but couldn't go against my mother's wishes. My premonition that it would be the end of my parents' marriage wouldn't go away.

I met Aunt Noreen in Grafton Street. I can still see her standing at the underwear counter in Newell's of Grafton Street, now a branch of Dunnes Stores. She was a handsome, sturdy, white-haired widow in late middle-age, with honest blue-blue eyes and a no-nonsense attitude. The modern term "tough love" applied to her relations with all young people, although it was unheard of as a phrase then. Noreen was one of life's Good Samaritans. I was the fourth young person she had helped: the others were nephews on her deceased husband's side.

She didn't talk much that day and I knew the cause: my mother infuriated her and my father still didn't have a job. Matter-of-factly she picked out sensible striped pajamas and also a girdle to hold up my stockings. I looked at it in dismay. Was I expected to wear this rubber armor? My mother believed girdles were bad for your muscles, so I didn't own one. I had hardly even worn stockings, mostly knee or ankle socks, or nothing, in the summer. I did wear a bra though.

That evening's dinner at Aunt Noreen's was served with beautiful plates and the right cutlery. In the polished dining room, she rang a little bell for the next course, brought in by her housekeeper. Niamh was at the table so Aunt Noreen was more talkative now. But there was still no mention of her daughter needing a sister. What was my mother talking about?

"I expect you to work hard and make something of yourself," Aunt Noreen said.

Niamh didn't mention a sister either, but seemed perfectly happy without one. The school donated a secondhand uniform—an ugly navy weekday dress, which all pupils were expected to wear for the whole term, without it being laundered. (We wore underarm dress shields, which were washable.) A new Sunday tunic had been ordered for me; luckily this was worn over a check blouse, which could be laundered. While Mount Anville had many uniforms, Rathfarnham had only two, plus a divided skirt for sports. Aunt Noreen gave me her late mother's pale blue dressing gown, which I loved. It was a connection to someone who had known my grandmother; I had always imagined her wandering the Land of Youth in search of her lost son. The ancient Celts believed the living and the dead were separated by thin veils, and so did I at that time.

Because of this grandmother's death, I had become my mother's mother. It was my job to look after her, so how could she agree to another boarding school? We had a good life despite my father's occasional fits, from which she did her best to shield us. We went to the library on Saturdays where she got extra books for me. I also read her free trial subscriptions to American magazines: *Ladies' Home Journal*, *Reader's Digest*, and the *Saturday Evening Post*. She bought me cold cream and pore grains for my acne, and we had girl-talk over cakes in Fuller's Café, and any time there was money she bought Whipped Cream Walnuts. And how could she work nights, if no one was at home with the kids? What if she left us while I was gone? Or died? Then we'd be done for. Either way, nothing would be the same again. I had to grow up and wear a girdle.

Back home that evening, my mother searched my face. "Well?"

I dropped the packages on the floor. "I don't want to go."

She took me in her arms. "Darling . . . with Daddy sick—it's best."

I couldn't stop crying.

"I know, darling."

In the years since that day, I've learned that life consists of partings. In the end we lose everything, so we must learn the art of letting go. Despite sending me away, I knew my mother loved me. She was the wise one in the King Solomon story.

I went to Rathfarnham a few days later. My first impression was of more long, polished corridors, again swept by lay sisters, worker bees who served the queens. After Mass that first morning, Mother Paulinus pulled me from the chapel line and introduced me to Mother Columbanus, the head of First School. "This is Mary."

I didn't want to be bullied again, so didn't object to her calling me that—my family did, although I had been Mary Rose in Mount Anville.

"Welcome, my dear."

Mother Columbanus taught the seniors. For the moment I didn't have much to do with her, but one day I would be in her class. She was slight, with olive skin and penetrating brown eyes, an inspiring English teacher who must have been a beauty as a girl. She was also an eccentric who later reminded me of Muriel Spark's Miss Jean Brodie because she had similar crazy notions, saying that people from Cork were imperialists, or girls who entered beauty competitions resembled elephants in a circus—this was a silly worry, for there were no candidates in the school for such a competition. I went into third year but, because of family problems, I was behind the others. I still knew no Irish, although the nuns didn't believe this. How had it happened? Maybe I was stupid?

Loreto schools have a special ethos. Sports and music were everything, and I wasn't good at either. There were two string orchestras and two choirs, but I couldn't sing or play an instrument, although the wonderful music penetrated even my tone deaf ears. Sports I considered anti-intellectual and hated. It was another school for the rich and more of a Gradgrind place than Mount Anville—exams and rote learning were very important. Any individuality was flattened out by the ugly uniform, so I didn't seem different. The library, beside the parlor, was only for seniors, although I found *John Halifax, Gentleman* somewhere, a Victorian novel by Mrs. Craik echoing our family's misfortune. There were other good things about the school: the food was better—a boiled egg wasn't an extra, and rashers were served twice weekly. If hungry, like Oliver Twist, you asked for more. Unlike him, you got it.

Like Mount Anville's, the atmosphere of Rathfarnham was cloistered. Correspondence was opened, except that from parents; the apex of happiness was a letter from home. We lived in a religious regime where everything was a sin. The curtained cubicles were called "cells." The girls exchanged holy pictures as a sign of friendship, reproductions of the Old Masters which you see today in museums, and we went to morning Mass and evening Benediction. Off our own bat, we made novenas and did the nine First Fridays for the

Holy Souls. I took the pledge, becoming the president of the Pioneer Abstinence Association, probably in reaction to my father, and, although not previously religious, I began to be now. It consoled me that another, better world was waiting. Then, one day, a retreat priest announced dramatically from the altar, "One day you will be in Heaven or in Hell!"—which frightened me into praying even harder. But later that year John XXIII was elected Pope, and everything was to change in the church.

I had come to the school mid-year but still made friends. Evening recreation was ballroom dancing in the gym to music from a record player in the corner. It didn't seem odd for two girls to dance together then. Girls got crushes on nuns or older girls, which was considered friendship rather than lesbianism, and wasn't discouraged by the nuns. On the whole I was happy, but worried about looking right. On the last day of term, we wore home clothes, embarrassing, because mine were American hand-me-downs, and everyone else's seemed stylish. It gave me a complex so for a while I made up stories that we had a Bentley. A classmate, whose father owned a garage, quizzed me, knowing this couldn't be true. A lie has to be believable: I should have picked an ordinary car, a Ford Anglia maybe. But these far-fetched fantasies, composed staring out of the study window, consoled me in those years.

I was returning from the loo one night when a flashlight was shone in my face. Feeling guilty for being out of bed, I hurried to my cell without stopping.

The next morning, the nun quizzed me. "What were you doing out of bed?"

I felt nervous. "I went to the bathroom."

She stared, as if I were lying. "Are you sure?"

"Yes."

"I think you were sleepwalking."

I shook my head, blurting. "It wasn't me."

Although I had no memory of it, I was told I had been in the study hall. Even worse, I had taken out books from my desk each night and read them. Then I had banged the desk shut and gone back to bed. I couldn't believe all this and feared exposure as some sort of a fraud. Instead, I was locked nightly into one of the nuns' corner wooden cells in our huge dormitory and given a chamber pot for emergencies. But I was afraid to use it in case the tinkling was heard. Later, as a senior, I always had to share a room, first with Niamh and then with others. But we all got on well and I got used to my role as a sleepwalker, believing that it gave me some melodramatic interest.

What kept me alive in those years were the old films shown on feast days: *I Remember Mama* and *A Tale of Two Cities*, starring Dirk Bogarde, still my favorite actor. For years, I was in love with either Dirk or Sydney Carton, I'm not sure which, but was attracted to the rakish type, who died for love of another. I knew the story of Robert Emmet and his love for Sarah Curran. He hadn't wanted an epitaph to be written until his country took its "place among the nations of the earth." The words inspired me and I wrote an essay on him for a competition, but got nowhere. Another treat was a visit to the Disabled Artists' Exhibition, where Christy Brown, then unknown, painted with his foot, ignoring our circle of gaping schoolgirls.

For my Intermediate Certificate, I was to read *Henry IV, Part I*, and was intrigued by the characters: Prince Hal and Hotspur were my pin-up boys. I was assigned a grinder for Irish, a nun who took me for a lesson every night, so I began to catch up. At Christian Doctrine class, I recited a hymn to the Holy Ghost, praying a bird would land on me, making me clever. In fifth year, Mother Columbanus taught us English, and her obsession with the character of Hamlet passed to me. Also her interest in Francis Ledwidge and his complete opposite, Dr. Johnson. Another of her obsessions was Milton, who had created the rebellious devils and knew he would be a famous writer at age seventeen. That idea of being a writer still intrigued me and I spent happy hours thinking of poetry and poets, especially Shelley, whose "Ode to the West Wind" was perfect for adolescence.

I fall upon the thorns of life! I bleed!
A heavy weight of hours has chain'd and bow'd
One too like thee: tameless, and swift, and proud.

We read no modern poetry or women writers, which then didn't even strike me as odd, although I had vaguely heard of Mary Lavin. Also my mother's family was connected by marriage to Kate O'Brien whose first novel, *Without My Cloak*, was supposed to have been based on them. Aunt Noreen's father, a passionate gardener, had been a model for one of the characters. I confided to a classmate that "the writer's sister was my mother's aunt by marriage." This convoluted relationship translated into her being *my* aunt. In English class one afternoon, when Mother Columbanus criticized Kate O'Brien's novel, *The Land of Spices*, which had been banned by the Censorship of Publications Act for the innocuous phrase "in the embrace of love," my friend yelled out, "She's Mary's aunt!"

Mother Columbanus stared at me in shock. The surprising thing, and an example of attitudes at the time, was that this nun, an intelligent woman with a deep feeling for literature, seemed to be completely on the side of the ban, which was the work of the Irish state rather than the Catholic Church. The same fate befell any Irish writer who was any good: Benedict Kiely, Seán Ó'Faoláin, Edna O'Brien. Being semi-related to a banned writer greatly improved my status. Also it meant that Kate O'Brien was no longer disapproved of in my presence. We didn't know it, but we lived in a theocracy, ruled by John Charles McQuaid, the tyrannical archbishop of Dublin. In the early 1960s, I had tried to buy *The Catcher in the Rye* in the Eblana Bookshop without success because it too was banned. And Mother Columbanus had once confiscated a novel by Henry James, which my mother had bought for me. It was a disappointment to learn later in life that he wasn't in any way salacious.

The best thing in that school was getting onto the debating team in fifth year—but we lost by a point to Bray, the winners that year. Another was discovering sports. I made the 3D netball team, consisting of the school rejects: the overweight, layabouts, and asthmatics. We surprised everyone by reaching the league final, which we unfortunately lost by a point or two. When I said it was "fate," the games mistress glared at me as if I were a traitor to my country—sports were taken seriously in Rathfarnham.

My three-and-a-half years passed happily. Like Tennessee Williams' Blanche DuBois, I remember the kindness of strangers in those years. I became friends with Máire, a brilliant pimply girl with glasses a year or so younger than me. Her mother was dead and this evoked my sympathy: I couldn't imagine living without mine. Máire and I were kindred spirits who both hated hockey so we began walking around the grounds after tea, avoiding the belligerent swans in the convent pond. Máire was another reader, and I was in awe of her knowledge of Marx and Lenin.

"All property is theft," she explained, a quote which fascinated me. Certainly property hadn't done our family any good. Máire also had a twist on Rousseau's famous maxim about freedom "Man is born free, and everywhere he is in chains" became "Man is born in chains, and his only freedom lies in his ability to rattle them." Later on she did psychology in university but died young in her early thirties, but all that was in the future. I was to remain at Rathfarnham until my Leaving Certificate, my longest time at any school. Others complain about boarding schools, but everything is relative. The rules gave me structure, security, and a fixed abode in term-time at least, thanks to Aunt Noreen. Although students weren't allowed out except for Saturday games, my mother was expert at arranging visits to the "dentist," when we would head for the pictures instead. And during Lent, when there was no tuck shop selling sweets, she visited, along with her bohemian Parisian cousin, a niece of her father's, who was married to a *New York Herald Tribune* reporter, bringing me chocolate. My mother didn't believe in fasting. I came to realize, even more, that having an American mother was different.

I was to remain in the school for another three years, until 1962. But after my first term, I went home for the holidays, resuming my role as a "Girl Guide." The situation wasn't any better there, although my mother always put the best light on things. But next time my parents had a major fight, she might leave for good.

Chapter Twelve

In the summer of 1959, Maurice and I went to Irish College, far away in northwest Donegal. It was arranged through our schools and, since I hadn't been asked for money, Aunt Noreen must have paid. The Loreto nuns were good about pretending things were normal when they weren't, and they had once provided my ticket to a Vienna Boys Choir concert in the Gaiety Theatre. My mother had continued to think that we should be exempt from learning our native tongue, but the upcoming Intermediate exam filled me with fear. Maurice was starting the Leaving course and had some sort of block too—worse than mine. But we both needed Irish to pass our exams. Since going to Rathfarnham, I had learned sample essays by heart and could take a mental snap of an Irish poem, then recall the lines, although I didn't always know what they meant. I had some sort of photographic memory. My problem with Irish was the absence of context. Years later I heard the story of Raftery, the Irish poet who had been blinded by smallpox, which killed all his siblings. If I had heard that story as a teenager, his poetry would have been much more relevant. It was the same with Latin and French poetry. We just learned off the lines by rote and knew nothing about the writers or their backgrounds.

The night before departing for Donegal, I brought my mother her tea on a tray. "You'll be OK without me?"

"Of course, darling."

I wasn't so sure: her answer had been too quick. There was a ritual about getting her ready for night duty since her white nursing coat always needed ironing, and she wore a starched nurse's cap. There were her usual instructions about putting the younger children to bed. Then I walked her down to the bus stop in Upper George's Street, waiting until her bus came. I hated us parting, even for a night. My mother hadn't ever left us for long—on her one trip to London, she had stood on the deck of the ferry, wishing she could swim back. And since that swim in Sandycove, I had thought this a possibility. But Irish College was only for a few weeks.

While my mother got more frantic about finances, our father got odder. He dressed up in his three-piece suit every day and had an obsession with washing his clothes and polishing his shoes. We had got used to his brain lesion by now, which caused headaches and made him "giddy." But there was no one to ask about it, so we never discussed it. We just knew that drink drove him mad, and when he did imbibe, he ranted about his pet hates. He couldn't cope with the endless bills, which my mother's meager salary didn't cover; it hardly kept us in food, and we supplemented our income by pawning anything left of value. Our father wasn't usually violent now, but could be if he was drunk. Luckily he couldn't afford the booze anymore, so he painted peacefully—more picturesque landscapes of Spain, or rowing boats in a harbor, or west-of-Ireland scenes similar to Paul Henry's.

Donegal was the farthest from home I had ever been, as our family didn't travel much. Maurice and I took the bus to Kingsbridge Station. We weren't close, but neither did we fight. We tolerated each other, separating by mutual agreement when seeing the other students on the platform. He went with the boys while I stood awkwardly with the girls, recognizing Vera, a Rathfarnham classmate. She was renowned for her home clothes and prowess on the hockey field. I can still see her sitting in study, red-faced and sweating from practice after tea. As I was a non-player, she had few words for me, saying only that I would never be as good a writer as Anne Frank.

Sheila Duggan ran the Irish College. A small, red-faced terrier of a woman with wild white hair, she wore a heavy tweed suit with a long baggy skirt. She frightened everyone, ticking names against a list.

"Máire Rós ní Cheallacháin!"

I told her I was there. "Anseo."

I sounded interesting in another language. Maybe I would use my Irish name? Then I could be someone else, because it was my fantasy to disappear. There were hugs and goodbye shrieks as we were marshaled onto the train by Sheila's assistant, a heartthrob called Dáithí, a tall, beautiful, godlike creature, who didn't notice me. How could he? Although I had a new dress with a starched underskirt and wore my new red duffel jacket—bought for me by Aunt Noreen's son—my ponytail was untidy and my nose not right. I'd caught a glimpse of it in a mirror and asked my mother if it could be fixed. She said not to be silly: it was just my awkward age.

From Sligo we took a bus to Gortahork, a straggling village with small fields and low stone walls. In the distance was Mount Errigal. On arrival, we were allocated to different houses, scattered higgledy-piggledy around. Maurice was sent one way; I went in the other direction, along with Vera and another classmate, Aisling, who was renowned for playing the cello. Our house was a new bungalow with a thistly field behind. The front garden was muddy, but the house was comfortable inside, with old-fashioned furniture and a big kitchen dresser with blue-striped plates. There was a lovely turf smell—which came from the cream-colored range, lit constantly, even though it was summer. We three girls shared a bedroom. To my relief, the others picked the double bed, so I had the narrow chair-bed to myself. Maybe they wouldn't notice that I didn't have the required baby-doll pajamas, but the sensible striped flannels Aunt Noreen had bought me. Two girls from the Royal School, Cavan, shared the house. I had never met Protestants except for the Fergusons next door, and looked forward to getting to know these housemates. Perhaps they were Girl Guides? My big regret was getting too old for camping.

On the first evening, Sheila Duggan blew into the house like the west wind. As she chatted in Irish to the Cavan girls, I was amazed at their fluency. I didn't know Protestants spoke Irish. Then she barked something at me. I didn't understand her, so Vera translated. "She wants to see our room."

We went in and Sheila pointed to my chair-bed. "Ceart go leor?"

I just looked at her.

"Ceart go leor?"

God, what was she saying? She looked about to explode.

I felt faint. "Eh—?"

"Is the bed all right?" she asked gently.

I felt myself go beetroot. "Yes—I mean—sea, sea."

I was amazed that she had inquired after my comfort. I have never forgotten this kindness from an overwhelmed woman with so many teenagers to look after. Then she stormed out of the house, barking "slán" at the Bean an Tí—goodbye to the woman of the house.

At breakfast, enjoying homemade brown bread, we sat at the kitchen table like a happy family. The Cavan girls were the same as us. The only difference was that they wore school blazers, even though it was the holidays, while we had home clothes. Unlike our neighbors, the Fergusons, these girls had no interest in the Queen or Princess Margaret, nor in the Girl Guides. Besides, they were diligent about speaking Irish while we Loreto girls, although meant to speak it in the house, cheated in our bedroom. One weekend a Cavan girl's brother visited. He was a Trinity College medical student who laughed and joked in expert Irish too. I was in love at last, but there was no hope: he was too old for me.

The days were full. After breakfast we made our beds, then went to classes, morning and afternoon. Maurice and I were in the same group—the most elementary. I soon found myself learning, in response to Sheila Duggan's drilling.

"Conas atá tú?" she snapped, asking how I was.

I didn't dare not answer.

"Tá mé go maith, go raibh maith agat," I rattled back, saying I'm fine, thanks.

Things began to make sense: Irish was a language like any other. It had verbs and subjects and present and past tenses. Incomprehensible bunábhars, learned by heart in school, were now understandable. They meant something—in this case, the summary of a poem. I was getting rid of my phobia about my native tongue.

Every evening we had céilís with "The Walls of Limerick" and other dances supervised by the divine Dáithí. After the first week, people began to pair off. The main question on everyone's mind: who would Dáithí ask up tonight? So far I hadn't been picked. Then a local boy liked me. One night we met by the stone wall at the edge of a field. He didn't want to talk, but he grabbed me and kissed me. I asked to go for a walk. "How long would it take to get to Mount Errigal?" He kissed me again, shaking badly. It was my first, under the shadow of the mystical mountain. Unfortunately I was more interested in the scenery, so things didn't progress. I had no boyfriends and knew nothing about sex. Any knowledge I had concerned the sex life of plants. I still thought reproduction had to do with French kissing, and was unsure of what went on between men and women.

At the end of the second week, I got a letter with an English stamp of the Queen's head. I recognized my mother's sloping, American handwriting. Where had she gone?

> *Darling,*
>
> *I'm in England. I hope you understand that I had no choice. I have to bring your father to his senses. Aunt Noreen has promised to pay any outstanding bills. I've got a job in a hospital in East Grinstead, so will be able to send money home. I'll be back to see you before school starts. I'll write again soon,*
>
> *Love, Mummy*

I stared numbly at the letter. The worst had happened. What did she mean, she'd be back before school started? She had got me out of the way and escaped. It had been a mistake to leave her alone. A big one.

"Is anything wrong?" Aisling asked.

"No," I lied, putting the letter into the envelope. Although we had become friends, I never talked about home

"You look pale."

"I'm naturally pale."

Why had my mother gone without telling me? She had planned it, obviously knowing I would never have let her go. But what would happen now? Who would pay the bills? What would we do for money without her salary? Who would keep the creditors at bay? Daddy wasn't able to cope, the boys couldn't stand stress, and I was fifteen.

I don't remember talking to Maurice about the letter. He tended to ignore things, hoping they would go away. My mother was right: boys were hopeless. Towards the end of the Irish course, a girl got a crush on him, inviting his whole house to a midnight feast. They all cycled to the other side of the village in the secrecy of the dark to celebrate going home in a few days. Unluckily, they were discovered and, worst of sins, heard speaking English. Maurice, who had stood his ground, was caught and sent home before me: it was the opposite of long ago, when children were punished for speaking Irish.

But our mother's departure overshadowed everything. This time our luck had run out.

Chapter Thirteen

My father didn't seem to miss my mother, but looked at me suspiciously on my return a day later. I guessed this was because of the midnight feast. Had I been up to something too? My brother's punishment was unfitting for such an innocent crime; even I knew that. I knew also that it had dawned on my father for the first time that I was now a teenager and capable of going astray. It was worse for a girl: everything was in the Ireland of the day. But he needn't have worried. I only liked unattainable types: film stars and men in books.

I had made friends with a waitress in a Dún Laoghaire café. Although we hadn't a penny, this job was considered infra dig by my father, who accused me of keeping bad company. Her boyfriend, also at the Irish College, had been found under the same bed as Maurice. That was how we met. Although she was an ordinary girl, doing an ordinary job, my father worried. But the concept of "teenager," which was spreading worldwide, didn't exist in our family. Up to this time my father was the hell-raiser; now he had been upstaged by his shy eldest son.

With my mother gone, my father depended on me, so I was in charge of everything again. But there was nothing left to sell or pawn, so we waited for my mother's weekly wire of money to buy food. It came on a Thursday when she was paid, and I cashed it immediately in Dún Laoghaire Post Office. But it was only six pounds and not enough for the household bills, all now in arrears.

Gradually things disintegrated: the electricity was cut off—the phone and TV had been gone for ages. There was no light to read by, no hot water or any way to cook, or even make a cup of tea. So I lit a fire in the dining room grate and cooked on that. We lived happily enough on porridge and bread and tea, boiling the kettle on the open flame. It was good practice for camping. I was some sort of Girl Guide at last. One day the chimney went on fire, and Mr. Ferguson ran in from next door with a wet sack. He managed to put out the blaze, but was too polite to comment on our unconventional cooking method.

My mother sent letters as well as wires from East Grinstead, where she had got the job as a nurse in a burns hospital. Every day I went down to the seafront and stared at the waves lashing the pier, or watched the mail boat going out, thinking she was on the other side of the water. I desperately wanted her back.

One day I asked at the ticket booth about the fare to England.

"What part of England?" the seller barked.

Of course, there were different parts. "I dunno . . ."

"North or south?"

"Eh . . . I'm not sure."

"*Where* do you want to go?"

"East Grinstead."

"You need a connection from London."

A connection? That would cost even more money, which I didn't have.

Despite everything, Dún Laoghaire was still lively. There were yachts, bands on the seafront, as well as a member of the landlord's Plymouth Brethren preaching on a Sunday night. I often stood, admiring his courage for declaring his Christian beliefs in public, a thing I couldn't do. I had no friends, but didn't have time for any, because housework and cooking took nearly all day. We still went swimming in Sandycove where you didn't need money and could sit all day on the beach, or paddle or swim. Bill Haley and His Comets, or Cliff Richard and the Shadows, sang from nearby transistors and we didn't seem any different from the other families. In the long summer evenings, Daddy took us for a walk on the pier, like a real father. He was in good form now, and didn't rant and rave, because he wasn't drinking. We watched the mail boat going out, packed with emigrants carrying parcels or cardboard suitcases to a new future. Back home, I read by candlelight in my dust-free bedroom—Georgette Heyer or Agatha Christie, still my favorites.

My father got vaguer and vaguer. He still spent days washing his own clothes, along with Freddie's. I did the rest in the bathtub, which was hard with no hot water. Dressed to kill, he had taken to cycling Evie's girl-sized bike, and even chatted with our neighbor Dr. Singer—that he was Jewish didn't seem to matter now. Like all my father's prejudices, this one had no reality and appeared only in drink. In May of that year the Shanahan Stamp scandal had broken, after a robbery of three hundred thousand pounds' worth of stamps. Dr. Singer was in the act of moving to a Foxrock mansion when he was charged with fraud. It had been all over the papers and locals talked of nothing else. But, despite his lifestyle of lavish parties, Dr. Singer made his home a hub for the neighborhood children. My sister Evie told me that he would dare them to roll headfirst down the stairs: the reward was sixpence.

Although she was never persuaded to try this, she had been once left behind while visiting their new house and was locked in accidentally. There was panic until she was found, but all ended well.

One day a stranger in a khaki raincoat knocked on the door and wouldn't go away. He insisted on coming into the house and sat down, along with his assistant, who wore a similar mac. I recognized them as bailiffs—they had come to Dubber once and taken all the cows from the paddock. Now the landlord had sent these same men to evict us. As his helper carried furniture out of the house to the side of the road, my father begged them to wait. We were about to be homeless and he turned frantically to me. "I'll ring Auntie Eva," he said.

Auntie Eva, an eccentric whom we hardly knew, still lived in my father's family home, a big empty house on the North Circular Road. She was the elder of his two sisters—the younger and kinder one, who had been my godmother, had died a few years earlier. Auntie Eva had never liked my father. This was to do with his being left better off than the rest of his family; then his illness, subsequent failure in business, and bad quarrel with his brother.

The bailiff agreed to a phone call.

My father and I squeezed into the green phone box on Royal Terrace, which smelled of stale cigarettes and sweat. Big coins clunked into the black box. He dialed: the number rang and was answered, so he pressed Button A.

But Auntie Eva wouldn't take us in.

"You've made your bed!" she snapped, hanging up. It wasn't surprising: we never saw her now, and anytime we had in the past, our father forbade us to eat anything in her house.

I saw my father's despair. "I'll ring Aunt Noreen."

She was the only hope. I discovered she was on holidays in Kilkee, so got the hotel number from her housekeeper.

We waited again, as the phone rang.

A voice said, "Press Button A," and the receptionist got Aunt Noreen to the phone. She wasn't enamored of my father and I expected her to be angry too, but she listened quietly, as I told her what had happened.

"I'll ring the landlord," she said at once.

My father came on the line then, promising to repay her out of his next Violet Hill rents. We always got the check at Christmas, so that year's was long spent. Aunt Noreen arranged a reprieve and the bailiffs left, so we had until the end of July to get everything ready. Then we children were to stay with relations for the rest of the holidays and my father would go his own way. During the next four weeks, he and I packed up the house, arranging for the furniture to go into storage. I washed and sorted clothes for my sisters and Freddie, trying to keep them cheerful. Olwyn was eleven, Evie nine, and

Freddie six. Maurice and Barry tell me that they were there too, so they must have been.

One day Uncle Ted, my father's other brother, visited us. He was a big blustery man who wore expensive clothes and drove a new car. I had never met him properly, but I knew who he was. Now he brought a food package, consisting of many packets of dried peas and a pound of Cleeve's butter. I wondered what to do with the peas. Despite our poverty, we had never eaten such an unappetizing thing. Did you boil them, or soak them first? You couldn't eat them as they were, I knew that, but thought it rude to ask.

A set of golf clubs was in the hall.

"I've advertised them in the *Herald*," my father said.

My uncle pretend-putted with one. "Don't sell them. You'll need them again."

I was grateful for this kindness. It was a hopeful thing to say.

"Here, love," he said, giving me money. "Take the kids to the pictures."

So we all trooped down to the Pavilion. I remember that summer as hot, but the sunshine only emphasized my unhappiness. Winter suited me better: then I could hide under the "blanket of the dark," a phrase I was to read later in *Macbeth*. On the last day of July the bailiffs returned to make sure we had left the house as ordered. But before the movers came and we were collected by relations, our stuff was put on the side of the road. I'd forgotten this, but my cousin Niamh told me it was so, as she came with Aunt Noreen to collect Freddie and me. We were to stay with them in their beautiful bungalow on the north side. My sisters went to other relations in Clondalkin, and my two other brothers stayed with a retired merchant navy captain in Killiney, the widower of Aunt Noreen's dead sister.

"Adversity will make you stronger," my mother wrote in a letter to me.

I suppose she was right. Friends today often accuse me of not expressing my feelings. But I have no hard words to write about my mother's actions at that time. I knew how difficult her life had become. The husband usually went to work in England, not the wife. But life had got too much and my mother had jumped ship, knowing her family would come to the rescue on the instigation of Aunt Noreen. There wasn't any social welfare in those days—at least, my parents didn't know about it. But, although Ireland was poorer, you didn't see people sleeping rough like now. Today people talk openly about things, and there's more help, although many people now find themselves on the street because of economic misfortune. Our family had experienced yet another theme in Irish literature: eviction. I think about it, walking past a homeless person today. If it weren't for Aunt Noreen, we would have been on the street, or sent to orphanages where bad things might have happened to my sisters and Freddie. It was a difficult time for our family, but you can get over anything. You can start again, no matter how often you have to move house. Rents were lower in the past, I know, but something always turns up. Life is always beginning anew. This was my mother's philosophy, and she transmitted it to us.

It's easy to remember events, but more difficult to recall how you *felt* on a particular occasion. Today I think how generous it is to invite someone into your home. Life was ordered with Aunt Noreen. She had a beautiful orchard with endless apples, and the family read books and played croquet and ping-pong. In the evenings there were card games of Rummy or Whist. Meals were regular, and for dinner we had homegrown vegetables because Aunt Noreen was a passionate gardener. But, although I was in a safe place and no longer had to worry about money, we had lost our own home. When would we get another? I was meant to be happier, but felt this sense of loss. Freddie missed his mother terribly, so I became a substitute. He had been my baby because I had looked after him when he was born, and for years when my mother was working. He loved dogs and would agree to go to bed only if Aunt Noreen's collie went with him. The two of us already shared a bedroom, so now we were three.

In September, Aunt Noreen and other relations clubbed together and sent the three younger children to a convent boarding school, chosen because it took small boys. My older brothers returned to their school and I went back to Rathfarnham with Niamh, where I missed Freddie and my sisters. It was sad to be separated, but couldn't be helped unless I changed schools again. At the time I was too stunned to suggest it. My father began his bachelor life in a hotel beside the Phoenix Park, where he had grown up.

Chapter Fourteen

For the next few years we yearned for a permanent home but rented for a month at a time during school holidays along the east coast from Bettystown to Bray, where rents were low. My mother stayed in England for about a year, returning for those holidays. The first Christmas after Dún Laoghaire, we got together in a Skerries rental. It was a two-story Georgian cottage with a musty basement, but near the seafront, within earshot of crashing waves. We were so happy to hear all about our mother's English adventures. At first she had stayed in Sussex with her Parisian cousin—the one married to the *New York Herald Tribune* reporter. From there she got the job in the Queen Victoria Hospital. The burns unit had been founded by Sir Archibald McIndoe, the New Zealand plastic surgeon who had operated on injured young pilots from World War II. "A man of hope, with a forward-looking mind," was written under his portrait in the hospital lobby, and the words inspired my mother ever after.

She used to say that she would never allow her hair to go gray. "Not as long as I can lift a hand to my head!" Now it had turned red because she had dyed it herself to save money, so my father kept giving out about this. He accused her of meeting other men, which I blocked out. Her passions were innocent: I knew that from a young age. Love was a game she played to get through life. Although she was lonely in England and obviously unhappy married to my father, she had never seriously considered anyone but him and if he didn't know that, he was an idiot. Like many women of her generation, my mother was a puritan. I was to find that out in later years, because she glared at me if I was ever out late. And when I asked why she hadn't explained the facts of life to me more fully, she said, "You were too innocent."

That Christmas I slept in the damp basement bedroom and got hooked on American bestsellers like Morton Thompson's *Not as a Stranger*, which I had already seen as a film. I read everything I got my hands on, indiscriminately. Once or twice Maurice and I caught the train into Dublin to the pictures but, like all good things, the holidays came to an end. We returned to lonely boarding schools, my mother to England, and my father to a miserable Leeson Park bed-sitter the size of a box-room, with a sink, electric kettle, and hot plate—the bathroom was in the hallway. I think the attractions of bachelor life were beginning to pall. He wrote to me regularly on those pre-stamped lettercards, telling me that Dr. Singer's stamp fraud case had gone well: he had been cleared on a technicality but had left Ireland for Canada. I was glad for his children's sake that he had got out of Mountjoy. My father also visited me in school, or we met in town for a pork chop with applesauce in the Green Cinema restaurant. I must have concocted another "dentist" ruse because going out was still forbidden.

My father and I were getting on better. He had a way of making you feel good about yourself; you were an attractive young woman, not an ungainly adolescent. With his sense of occasion, he was right out of James Joyce's *Ulysses*. I have only to read it and he comes alive again. Things gave him "the willies," an expression found in Joyce, and, like many Dubliners, he was musical and fond of opera. When I was a teenager, he had often brought me to the Rathmines and Rathgar Musical Society to see operettas like *The Merry Widow*, and he encouraged my love of drama. I saw my first plays with him in Dún Laoghaire's Gas Company Theatre. I was delighted by them, and more so to be considered old enough for coffee at the interval. Throughout our childhood, he often brought my siblings and me to the pictures, where there were long lines for the matinée, but there was no question of us queuing. He simply walked the six of us into the lobby and tipped the doorman. We got the best seats too and once—as an added bonus—won the raffle in the interval: a crate of 7UP, then new on the market.

A few years ago a cousin told me my mother had married a "drover." I was shocked by this description, for my father was anything but. As well as Dubber, he had inherited two other farms, one of which had been compulsorily purchased by the Land Commission. There was also Violet Hill. He was potentially wealthy the day he met my mother in the train. "A gentleman but also a gentle man," Aunt Noreen once called him when we were speaking about him.

That year's Hill rent had been promised to Aunt Noreen for helping us out in Dún Laoghaire, but instead of repaying her, my father used it for holiday expenses, rent, and food. With what was left over he bought a small, black, battered Fiat. He was hoping to work for Uncle Ted, who was also in the cattle business. He needed a car to drive to country fairs: he had to get back in the swing. He also needed it for us. My sisters recently reminded me that they were to be fostered out that first Christmas after the eviction, but our father arrived at the school in the little black car at the last minute. "I've come for my children," he said, and the nuns had to agree to release them.

One day, when I was back at school after Christmas, Aunt Noreen came and asked to see me. This was a surprise, since she usually just visited Niamh. But when I went into the parlor, where she was wearing her fur coat, her face was set in anger and she immediately sent Niamh away. Then she began to scold me about my father's dishonesty. What had he done with the Violet Hill rent? He had promised it to her.

I stammered something about buying the car.

"Why didn't you tell me?"

I didn't know why. I should have told her, but how could I?

She got angrier and angrier. "You've turned into a double-crosser like your parents."

Her words stabbed me. I began to cry. I wasn't a cheat.

"Stop that crying!"

I couldn't. "Sorry, Aunt—"

"Don't call me Aunt!"

She said this when she was mad. Normally she accepted that "aunt" was a generic term for an older female relative or a friend of your parents, but by now she had had terrible rows with my mother, who regularly sent unkind letters to her as well as to other relations. In one bad row, our mother had been turned from Aunt Noreen's door. I sat there, thinking of all this, until Niamh returned. Then, swallowing back tears, I went back to study. The study hall was always bleak after tea, but that day it was worse. I stared blindly at my book, unable to take anything in.

I must have blocked out the fact that my father was to repay her, but, either way, I had no control over him or his finances. Aunt Noreen was about sixty then. I now understand how infuriating it must have been to have had to bail out our family so often. It was no joke, having to cope with two incapable parents and six children, all with expensive needs: school uniforms, shoes, dressing gowns, pajamas. Noreen was wealthy, but not that wealthy. She had been good to us, and probably thought I was ungrateful, which wasn't true. I was the buffer state between her and my parents, and I burned with the injustice of being wrongly blamed. It wasn't fair: I wasn't a double-crosser. I loved my parents, and my first loyalty was to them. They were poor things, but my own.

Chapter Fifteen

It was midsummer; tar melted on the roads.

"Blast it!" my father cursed, as our small black Fiat, with its overloaded trailer, swerved to one side of the road. We had got a flat tire when leaving the town of Rush in County Dublin. It was embarrassing because we were flitting from a rental there, without paying. Now we would probably be caught. My father got out of the car, found the spare wheel in the boot, and frantically started changing the wheel. I stood by the roadside, worriedly watching to see if the landlady was following us. No one yet.

My mother had a new job in the Skin and Cancer Hospital in Hume Street. While she was at work and my brothers were sent ahead by train with the younger children, I, as usual, had packed our stuff into the trailer and tidied the house with my father. What we were doing wasn't honest, but necessity knows no law. We had no money, although the monthly rent was only sixteen pounds. I remember that distinctly.

A car slowed beside us. God, don't let us be caught, I prayed.

"Need a hand?" the driver asked.

What if he was the landlady's husband? I studied his face, wondering if I had seen him before. My father looked from the other side of the car, red-faced. "I can manage, thanks."

But the man insisted on helping and waved us off a short time later. "You'll be OK now!"

As we drove on towards Dublin, my father lit a cigarette and my heart calmed down. Our destination was Harcourt Terrace, near the center of the city. By some miracle, my parents had rented a second-floor flat in No. 7, a decaying pillared Palladian mansion in mid-terrace. Nearby was the Grand Canal with swans, ducks, and leafy trees, a beautiful place to walk. The house was meant to have once sheltered the rebel Lord Edward FitzGerald but was now owned by Miss McGeehan, a gaunt, retired Donegal schoolteacher, big in the Legion of Mary. Our existence couldn't be hidden because she lived in the ground floor flat which we passed by as we went in and out. No landlady, when renting accommodation, ever wanted *six* children, but she had taken pity on us. I don't know how we paid the rent there because my mother soon became ill with a bleeding ulcer and couldn't work.

Maurice had been farmed out to country cousins, but Barry stayed with us that summer, getting a job in Bacon Shops of Talbot Street, which was owned by another relation. Olwyn, then twelve, helped another, who ran a knitting factory in the mews behind her Merrion Square home. I, as usual, looked after the others and my father: cooking, washing, and cleaning. I didn't resent this at all. Actually, I quite liked managing the family. It gave me a sense of importance, and I got more practice in cooking which I have loved ever since.

Our relations arranged credit in Lipton's of Grafton Street, where we were allowed ten pounds a week for food. It's little by today's standards, but in 1960 it was considered enough for a big family. The manager, Mr. Norton—father of the famous actor, Jim Norton, and his acting teacher sister, Betty Ann—had known my mother when she was young, when Mr. Norton had worked for one of her uncles. At first I was daunted by him because he had a cast in his eye which made him look severe, but we became friends, as he advised me on what groceries were the best value. I usually got pork chops and a chicken for the weekend, which could be put on the account. Sometimes I broke out and made a steak and kidney pie. There was no fridge in the flat, so Sunday's dinner often smelled high, but I cooked it anyway. No one ever got sick. What the mind can't see, the heart, or stomach in this case, can't feel. And cooking kills all bugs.

I still had asthma and often walked through the early morning city, waiting for a chemist to open, where *Do-Do* tablets could be got without prescription. They contained ephedrine, which was some sort of high and made my heart thump, but it was a relief to be able to breathe freely again.

The landlady once took me to a Patrician Meeting, a discussion group run by the Legion of Mary. It was stimulating and I met people to chat to. But mostly I took the two younger children to Stephen's Green or we visited my mother, now a patient in Hume Street Hospital where she had recently nursed. Her cousin, a consultant with influence there, had ordered rest, so she had a small attic room.

Our flat was grand but bare, and I imagined us as a family in post-revolutionary Moscow. There were two big bedrooms and a huge drawing room with a marble mantelpiece. The kitchen and bathroom were in the jerry-built extension which went up the back of the house, serving each story. There were plug-in electric heaters and a fireplace for the winter months.

A few houses from us lived Micheál MacLiammóir, the English actor who, with his partner Hilton Edwards and Lord and Lady Longford, had cofounded the Gate Theatre in Dublin. I had seen him playing Iago in the film version of *Othello*. He was a well-known homosexual, which at the time was against the law and considered a terrible sin, yet Dubliners always accepted him and his partner. When occasionally passing him in the street, as he walked towards the canal, I stared curiously at his makeup and luxurious camel-hair coat, thinking it must be the garb of actors and the makeup must be for the next performance. I knew MacLiammóir was famous and that celebrities visited him regularly. Taxis pulled up outside his house, and rich voices called warmly to each other in the summer night. If only I could go on the stage or do something artistic, I thought. The only trouble was I couldn't act.

Once looking vaguely puzzled as I stared at him, Mícheál tipped his trilby to me. Oh glamour, and only a few doors away! But I was stuck in my own mundane existence. As usual the housework took all day, but I had time for reading at night. I always had time for that.

One day the bell went. I ran downstairs. A well-dressed, middle-aged woman was at the doorstep. "Is your mother in?"

I said no.

Her face was like thunder. "I got your address from your Uncle Ted." Uncle Ted was a well-known businessman and lived in Skerries in a big house near the harbor.

"You rented my house in Rush."

I prayed for the ground to open.

"I want my money!" she said.

"My mother's out."

"Out spending other people's money!"

"No, she's in hospital—very ill."

Instead of scolding me more, the woman broke down and cried. "If you knew how hard we worked on that house."

I felt like crying too. "I'm sorry. I'm very sorry."

The woman left. I don't know if she ever got paid.

Aunt Poll, my maternal grandmother's elder sister and then a distinguished old lady near the end of her life, visited my mother when she got out of hospital. She didn't come into our flat, but parked outside in her chauffeur-driven car. My mother sat in with her, introducing me, as I stood on the pavement. "She's like Jim," my great-aunt said immediately. This was our American grandfather.

Afterwards I asked my mother about Aunt Poll.

"I lived with her when I first came to Ireland. She invited us to dinner when I got engaged to Daddy."

My mother told me the story. Aunt Poll, a widow, lived in Milltown with a daughter who had had a play performed in the Abbey Theatre. The house had been impressively grand and all the furniture antique. Good china and heavy silver cutlery were on the Irish linen tablecloth. There would have been sherry first and several dinner courses, as well as wine. My father was being vetted as suitable husband material.

"I believe you're a farmer?" my great-aunt inquired during dinner, appraising my father's expensive suit. She always wore black, in mourning for her own husband, who had died young.

My father nodded. "I buy cattle and graze them."

Dublin was small and everyone's lineage was known. "*Who* is he?" was asked of boyfriends even in my time.

"You're related to the Callaghans—the harness shop of Dame Street?" Aunt Poll inquired.

"No. We're North Circular Road."

The Liffey divided Dublin society then, as it still does.

She cleared her throat, "Hm . . . I don't know of your family. Well, so long as you can support my niece."

He laughed. "I hope to."

My mother's Jesuit uncle had also asked about my father's suitability, but everyone at the Dublin cattle market had vouched for him, according to Aunt Noreen. We visited that uncle from time to time. But it was the first and last time I ever saw this great-aunt. She was my mother's aunt. When I was young, I didn't think much about this, but now that I'm an aunt myself, I find it odd. It was good of her to vet my father, but why didn't she take more interest in my mother's life? Aunt Noreen was only a first cousin, yet she had always shown concern for our family.

At the end of the summer, we all went back to our different schools. I went into fifth year, having got four honors in my exam. My marks surprised me, especially because I had learned Irish from scratch since going to Rathfarnham. The following Christmas holidays, we were still renting Harcourt Terrace. Our noisy tribe had piled back from boarding school, laughing and screaming at the top of our lungs and no doubt upsetting the other residents. Benedict, a Nigerian student, lived in one of the chilly attic flats at the top of the house. You hardly ever saw black people in Dublin then, and mostly they were at university, so Benedict seemed exotic. People then didn't think of Africa as being hungry. It was a continent to convert, the home of the missions, cuddly black babies, and Benedict. He had coal black skin and eyes that glittered in the dark. I had often passed him on the stairs without stopping. His greeting was an unvaryingly formal, "How do you do?"

I always turned away shyly. What was he staring at?

My parents invited him for Christmas Day because he was so far from home. My mother, by now recovered from her illness, had arranged to work through the holiday and, by hook or by crook, everyone would get a present. Although the Violet Hill rents had been already spent that year, there were clothes and books for us older ones and toys for the youngsters. I can still hear Freddie nagging: "Am I getting my train set?" My mother would only hum tantalizingly. With her, hope always triumphed over experience: she would provide somehow.

That year Auntie Ellen had sent the money for my raincoat, the same as Audrey Hepburn wore in *Roman Holiday*. Like a sensible person, I was waiting for the sales. There was now only the dinner to buy, for which my mother would use her salary check. But on Christmas Eve morning, she came home looking tired out. "I'm afraid they didn't pay me."

"Didn't you ask them?" I said.

My mother took off her coat and scarf. "It horrifies me that a child of mine would expect me to dun people for money."

"Asking isn't dunning them!"

"It's hardly the spirit of Christmas. . . . We'll have to use your money."

I groaned. "What about my raincoat?"

She poked me in the ribs. "I'll find money for that."

I was fed up. "You'll borrow it, I suppose."

"Well, sharper than a serpent's tooth."

I wasn't sharp at all. As always, I was being out-generaled by my mother. It was no use. After all, we had to have a turkey and the trimmings. And there was the matter of Benedict: he was expecting a dinner.

In those days, Findlaters of O'Connell Street still delivered. We had always gone there because they had all the necessities: a turkey, smoked ham, a Thompson's pudding, Club Orange, and a tin of Jacob's *Afternoon Tea*. I watched resignedly as the blue-coated assistant stuffed my money into a little casket, which was carried by a wire to a cash desk on high. Goodbye, dear money. Goodbye, raincoat. And later the change disappeared into another flying casket in Clerys, where we stopped for last-minute tree decorations. My mother never left money unspent.

On Christmas Day, she caught up with sleep, while Barry and I cooked the dinner; by midmorning we had everything in train. The ham was boiling away, the turkey stuffed and sizzling, the potatoes peeled, the sprouts ready, and the tinned asparagus opened. There was only the pudding to be heated and the brandy butter to be whipped.

Benedict knocked on the door.

He was small and black, with a head appearing turtle-like out of a long drab overcoat. A bunch of flowers almost dwarfed him. He was probably quite young, but to me anyone at the university was ancient. Smiling, he gave me the flowers.

I reddened in delight, as Barry drew him manfully in.

No one had ever given me flowers before. I put them in a vase on the white marble mantelpiece, and went back to the cooking. When everything was ready, we called my mother. Then we all sat at the carefully laid table under the gaudy paper decorations that trailed from each corner of the ceiling. My father said grace and carved the turkey. Then I served the vegetables while my elder brother poured the drinks. There was the usual Club Orange for us, and a bottle of wine for my parents and Benedict.

I was next to him. As soon as I sat down, a hand clutched my knee. I pushed it away, glaring at him. He just smiled dazzlingly, showing his brilliant white teeth.

When we started eating, he talked about Africa. Yes, he had been educated by the Holy Ghost Fathers in Nigeria. Yes, he found Ireland lonely. And cold, very cold, although the Irish were warm and friendly. Hadn't he made new friends today?

He smiled and pinched my knee again.

As my mother served the pudding, he kept on touching me. This time I beat him off.

"What are you doing?" my father asked me suspiciously.

I waved my serviette. "Eh . . . just dropped this."

He gave me a curious look.

During the coffee Benedict stood up, taking the napkin out of the V-neck of his jumper. "I wish to thank you all very, very deeply. Also . . . I wish to explain . . . in my country the customs are different." He looked directly at me.

I wondered if they groped hostesses there.

He held up his glass. "I now would like to toast this family . . . for such generous hospitality."

I raised my glass. What else could I do?

After dinner my mother went to bed. My father smoked his Christmas cigar and chatted to Benedict and my elder brother. The lovely aroma wafted into the small jerry-built kitchenette, where Barry and I stacked the dishes. We would finish the washing-up later.

Imagination is memory, someone has written. Were we really as happy? Or is it just another memory of a memory? We always had good Christmases. And it was interesting to meet Benedict, despite his over-friendly habits. I don't know what became of him. Presumably he got his degree and went back to Nigeria, but I often wonder if he got caught up in his country's civil war.

We lived in that flat for only another few weeks. Since we were unable to pay the rent, the landlady moved us to the basement. My siblings had gone back to school and my mother was on night duty, so it was my task to help my father pack up yet again. When the two of us squeezed into the suicidal dungeon, it seemed to represent the nadir of all our misfortunes. I had never before shared a bedroom with my father, but now there was no choice. I could pretend to be camping again, but it wasn't so easy for him.

For the following Easter holidays, we were caretakers of 6 Harcourt Terrace, the adjoining house, which was vacant and for sale. It was another four-story mansion and impossible to heat. I don't remember the exact circumstances of that holiday time, only that an intruder stole our father's clothes from his bedroom wardrobe. We later discovered that the thief was sleeping on the top floor, but luckily we never met him.

Miss McGeehan sold No. 7 to the Legion of Mary after us. Next it was a home for battered wives, then it remained deserted for years. The windows were bricked up, mottled patches of damp covered the front pillars, and weeds choked the gravel. But somehow it was saved by the Celtic Tiger's boom years and converted into an architect's office.

Chapter Sixteen

Our next semipermanent stop was Bray, the seaside town where I now live. Since leaving Dún Laoghaire, we had booked into B&Bs there for several short school breaks. Now we began a longer stay of about two years, and saw Telefís Éireann come on the air on New Year's Eve 1961. Crowds cheered in O'Connell Street and celebrities like Micheál MacLiammóir and Siobhán McKenna spoke at the launch. I was glued to the screen.

My mother had rented a set for us to watch while she was at work, and we feasted on more cowboys: *The Virginian* or *Have Gun—Will Travel*. I don't remember my father being there, so maybe he was back traveling to buy cattle for Uncle Ted—he had a job doing this from time to time. At the time we were living in the top flat of a house called "Watergate" on the Meath Road. Years later, when the Richard Nixon scandal broke, I wondered at the coincidence. It seemed like plagiarism to steal our house name.

We had arrived in a taxi from Amiens Street Station the previous August, having got the train from a summer rental in Bettystown where we had to leave the donkey behind—crazily, our father had bought one for Freddie, who loved animals. The new landladies, although ancient, didn't object to the eight of us and our heavily pregnant dog, Susie, trooping around above them. I remember them today whenever I pass the house. It was a happy time and Bray reminded me of Dún Laoghaire, giving me, along with my mother, a lifelong love of seaside places. At night we used to walk the Esplanade and in daytime the Cliff Walk, as far as Greystones. We went on picnics to Kilmacanogue or rode the bumpers on the seafront. There were drawbacks to living in Bray, however: commuting for one. It was decades before the DART (Dublin Area Rapid Transit) service began and the trains were infrequent, so my mother took the bus into Dublin to work and was permanently tired.

At this time she started taking pills. She had charmed a Bray chemist, who supplied her with Preludin, a diet pill, which enabled her to stay awake on night duty. It was the worst thing for her, but the drug wasn't considered harmful then and many people took it, including the Beatles. On a few occasions, if she wanted the housework done, she gave her older children one each. "Giddyups," she said, dispensing them. We were filled with energy and suffered no ill-effects. Later my mother graduated to Dexedrine, also popular at the time, which took away her appetite and made her jittery, and then, of course, she had to take pills to sleep when she came off duty. Although she needed fewer hours sleep than others, it was the beginning of her undoing.

We were still in Bray the summer I left school.

By now we had moved to a bungalow on the Sidmonton Road, owned by an old lady in a nursing home. It was another happy time, with the plonk of cricket balls and other sounds of summer as boys from a nearby school played games. I made jam with raspberries from the garden and read *Wuthering Heights*, which Maurice had won as a school prize. Then Mother Columbanus sent me my Leaving Certificate results, saying she had hoped for something more spectacular. Oddly my best academic mark was Irish, although my oral exam had been borderline; the other marks were lower, owing to my spending a few weeks in hospital with a burst appendix just before the exams. I had gone through an adolescent rebellion against the nuns and hadn't worked hard enough in fifth year. I still passed everything, getting honors in domestic science and art, and had enough subjects, including maths and Latin, to do anything I wanted. There was no points system then—all you needed was your checkbook.

My mother wanted me to go to university. This irritated Aunt Noreen, who had arranged for a commercial course in one of the Loreto Colleges. She wanted me to earn my living as a typist and to go the National College of Art and Design at night. She was impressed with my drawing ability, but I still wanted to be a writer. Could this happen if I worked in Guinness' or a bank, my mother wondered? Of course, it might have, but at the time I was dominated by her.

"Aunt Noreen won't speak to me if I don't do it," I argued.

"I won't speak to you if you do!"

Throughout our childhood my father had liked to point out monuments and places of interest as we drove around Dublin. We had often passed the Parnell statue at the end of O'Connell Street, and my mother was fond of quoting its famous inscription: "No man has the right to fix a boundary to the march of a nation. No man has the right to say to his country, 'This far shalt thou go and no further.'" She recited this dramatically now, so I told Aunt Noreen I wasn't taking up her offer, but going to college. She wrote back that she was folding her tent and disappearing like the Arabs in the desert.

It was a miserable time. My life had the ingredients of a fable: the fairy godmother, the jealous mother. I was Cinderella; all I needed was the handsome prince. I turned down a year in France too, because it was in another convent—I had spent the last three-and-a-half years in one. Besides, I was under my mother's spell and felt I couldn't leave her at that point, but I always regret not learning to speak French fluently.

We had to leave Sidmonton Road for the usual reasons, but had nowhere else to go. It was time to search the newspapers' "For Rent" columns again. I saw an ad for a house in the *Evening Herald* and pointed it out to my father.

It was one of Ireland's few wooden houses. The row of four still stands at the crossroads of Upper and Lower Kilmacud Roads, Stillorgan—between heaven and hell, I thought back then. Heaven was the country garden, with its red peony roses, sloping down to tall trees which had been there when we came. Afterwards the roses were dug up and trees chopped down to widen the road for the nonstop suburban traffic—that noise was the hell bit. But it was a hell I knew, and the mind is its own place. The rent was only three pounds a week and it didn't say anything about children. Six were still a definite impediment, so my father drove to Cork where the landlord lived, telling him that he had only two offspring—Maurice and me.

"A bun and a brae is all ye need. A place to hang yer hat." The kindly Scot was charmed by my father, who could talk anyone into anything. That man, although he didn't know it, saved us from more years of wandering—we were now back in luck and had a real home with a garden and a proper address, instead of a flat or a B&B. I named the house "Shelley" after my favorite poet. We fixed it up, getting our furniture out of storage, although everything looked sadder and shabbier than we remembered and one-half of the mahogany dining room table had been stolen. But we were happy that the Scottish landlord lived so far away and we all squeezed into the three bedrooms: a girls' room, a boys' room, and a skimpy box-room for my parents. My mother had that by day, while my father had it by night.

The previous tenant, a Hungarian refugee who was going to England for work, offered us her "furniture"—orange boxes, for which she demanded ten pounds.

To my alarm, my mother gave her the money.

"You paid for junk!" I said.

"For luck, darling. That poor woman needs it."

So did we. If my mother gave everything away, how would we manage? She also had a habit of leaving tips, when we were barely surviving ourselves. It was her "bread on the water" philosophy of life, which she quoted now. I made a face, imagining soggy crusts washed up by the tide, but she was unrepentant.

"No one likes a mean person. She's a refugee, starting a new life."

All her life my mother had an ability to love others. She told us that if you met a beggar, you had to give whatever coin was first found in your pocket, even if it was a half-a-crown rather than a penny.

Our house hunting was over for the moment, but there were further worries on the horizon. Around this time, my mother started her shopping sprees. I usually went with her, to keep her safe. She bought clothes for all of us, but focused on me more than on the others. It all started because Aunt Noreen bought me an oversized green tweed cowl-neck coat. I hated fashion because it was something I could never keep up with. The coat was OK: it kept me warm and that was enough. It was good of Aunt Noreen to buy it for me. But my mother was furious and kept saying how hideous it was. I couldn't go to college in that, she insisted; I had to be properly dressed.

One day she dragged me into Switzer's of Grafton Street to get a suit. We looked at a few and I finally tried on a red Chanel number, while she perched on a tall stool.

"I like it!" she said, as I came out of the changing room.

I looked at myself in the mirror, while the assistant stared. It wasn't me; my mother must be mad. The skirt was too tight and would make it impossible to run for a bus.

"It really suits you," the assistant said.

She only wanted a sale.

"We'll take it," my mother said. "And a hat. Do you have a hat?"

An idiotic black pillbox was found. I tried it on, swearing inwardly never to wear it. The clothes were from my mother's youth, for someone in a magazine or a model on a ramp, not for an ordinary person like me.

"Great!" my mother said to the assistant. "You can wrap them."

"Mummy," I hissed, "when would I wear it?"

It was no use.

I took off the suit in the changing room and came out to find her smiling at the assistant, now back behind the counter. "Young people today have no sense of fashion. These are on account, by the way."

"Yes, madam."

And my mother gave a relative's name and address.

I glared at her. This was new.

"It's the easiest way to cope with my daughter's birthday."

"Yes, madam," the assistant said. "I'll just check the account." And she hopped off in the direction of the stairs.

The minutes stretched out in agony, but my mother was undaunted. She sauntered coolly about, stopping at a rail of coats and frowning over the price. Now was the time to run for it. I paced as far as the stairs and looked down at the shop floor. How could we escape? I was pretty sure my mother had no permission to use the account. We were done for. We would end up in prison.

I walked back to my mother. "I don't want them."

She pretended not to hear me.

"I said, I don't want them."

But she only smiled brightly.

My heart started to gallop as the assistant came back up the stairs. At the top, she stopped to talk to a tall, stripe-suited manager. As they started over, I frantically looked at my mother. Poking in her handbag, she took out a lipstick and coolly put it on.

"This is a little unusual, madam," the manager said.

My mother wasn't cowed. "What's so unusual?"

He coughed politely. "Ah . . . perhaps, we could ring to verify it."

"Certainly verify it!" My mother gave the relative's name.

"It's just a formality," he said, padding off towards the stairs.

The girl was busy behind the counter and I looked at my mother. She was pale and her upper lip was trembling, as it did when she was stressed. Oh, Angel of God, why had she done this just to get something I didn't want?

When the manager came back, his face was expressionless. "I'm afraid there was no answer. Would it do if we delivered them tomorrow?"

My mother pursed her lips.

"Our van delivers daily. If you give the assistant your address, we can have them out in the morning."

"That'll have to do," my mother said, leaning over the counter. "Shelley."

"The Chalet," the girl wrote.

"No. Shelley, as in poet. S-H-E-L-L-E-Y."

"The Shelley," the girl scribbled, flustered.

My mother sighed. "My daughter's literary. She named the house."

Usually I got mad when she told people things like that. But nothing terrible was going to happen now. We got out of the shop without being arrested and, strangest of all, the suit and hat were delivered the next day in a big box tied up with string.

The whole thing made me anxious. I should have stopped my mother, but she was a stronger person. What would happen when our relative found out? On top of that, I had no money for university fees. I had also fallen out with Aunt Noreen and was miserable about upsetting her by not doing the typing course. It looked as if I was ungrateful, but I was balancing on a tightrope. My mother was adamant: I was going to college and that was that. I had always wanted to attend an American university, so she wrote to one of her old beaus, suggesting that he pay for me. It didn't work, so she urged me to do Medicine in Dublin. But I wanted to study English: you had to read books to write one, and somehow I was determined to be a writer.

Chapter Seventeen

That October my mother opened a bank account in Stillorgan, having assured the manager about her salary. As soon as we got home, she wrote a check for my college fees. The account was a ruse and, of course, she was now overdrawn. But the manager, intrigued by my mother and worried that I would be embarrassed, honored the check. It was a kinder time than now, but my mother continued on her slippery financial slide.

She went on getting me things I didn't need: hideous stilettos and exotic bras—either without permission on relative's accounts, with dud checks, or even on her own account in Walpole's, the old-world Suffolk Street shop whose ancient attendants seemed to remember my grandmother from 1919. Clothes were important to my mother and it irritated her that I had no sense of fashion. How was I her daughter? How would I ever attract a man? I was young and should be living life. Why was I so shy, with my nose always in a book? She didn't understand her children at all.

That year the world hovered on the brink of disaster because of the Cuban missile crisis, but I was hardly aware of it. I had too many problems at home. I had started First Arts but soon dropped out, arranging to switch to Medicine the following year. I had changed my mind about Arts when I read *The Night They Burned the Mountain* about Dr. Tom Dooley and his mission to Vietnam. Many writers had also been doctors. Besides, Medicine was still my mother's wish and she wanted me to get a proper profession: she couldn't see the point in going to college to read books that you could check out of a library. I had never even been to the college library, but had foolishly spent all my money on the history department's reading list, which could have been borrowed. I could afford only the first three books.

To prepare for pre-med, I spent the rest of the year slogging at physics and chemistry, while enduring gropes from my grinder, an ancient old gentleman called Mr. Templeton. He had a chintzy bed-sitting room in Pembroke Road, just across from the house where my mother was born. As I bent over the physics tome, he would lean against me and next thing was tweaking my bra strap or pinching my bottom. When I pulled away, he would smile benignly. He was slight, with bright, china blue eyes. It occurred to me that he was acting improperly, but I accepted this behavior as normal. It was just the way men were—their passions were uncontrollable, even when they were so old. We'd been told that in school, and it had happened to me before. A nun had sent me for advice to a priest who exposed himself, so I had never returned or even told anyone—especially not the nun. But Mr. Templeton was genteel and always polite. After the grind, he told interesting stories about his time in the colonies, over biscuits and tea in blue china cups that matched his eyes. He seemed to know everything and offered grinds in all subjects except Irish.

I got my first job as a night attendant in St. Kevin's Hospital, situated in James Street, Dublin. Nowadays the name is changed to St. James' Hospital, but in the old days it was almost a workhouse, set in extended grounds. Nursing would be practice for my medical career and the money was good, so I spent the next summer there, helping to bed down the geriatrics. Many had broken hips, with legs hanging out of pulleys. Their bedsores were horrible and a sweet smell that must have been gangrene permeated the ward, although I did not know it then. One old woman wanted to use her own teacup, but wasn't allowed to by the sister in charge.

"She wants her tea in this," I explained to my superior.

"Use the hospital cup. She has notions about herself," I was told.

"But it's her own cup," I protested.

"Do as you're told, or you'll be sacked."

Part of my job was to wake the young doctors on night duty when there was an emergency. I had to carry a phone over to their residence, plug it in, and put it in their hand, making sure they didn't go back to sleep—there were never any girl residents then. An older woman attendant, who worked with me, sometimes went in my place. It was a relief when she did because I found it hard to be assertive with the groggy students. The older attendant and I got on well, although there was a definite pecking order between the registered nurses and us attendants. On one occasion I sat down to my sandwich at their table and was told to move. "You can't eat with us," a nurse said, as I tried to take in what she was saying. "You have to go to the scullery."

It was Irish apartheid.

The Monsignor, our former parish priest from the country, had always supported my mother, giving her advice about her rocky marriage. For years he had lent her books, which she passed on to me—a life of Talleyrand and books by French philosophers such as François Mauriac. In my religious phase I had asked the Monsignor for a copy of the Index, a list of banned books, but he was a liberal and told me to read anything I wanted. When he had visited my mother in St. Michael's after her hysterectomy, I couldn't believe the way he laughed at her jokes. I wondered would anyone ever laugh with me like that. Since she was such an incurable romantic, this had become another harmless infatuation on her part, which he indulged by coming now and again to afternoon tea. My mother had bought a special teapot and china for the occasion. She needed something to keep her going, she said; every woman did. Being in love was essential, and she always came home from work with stories about Mr. X or Mr. Y, patients who were "hanging on by their eyelashes." There would be a "one" for me too, she promised. He would appear someday soon, when I least expected it. I would run into him, or he'd be sitting "across a crowded room."

It didn't happen like that. I saw Rory on TV. He was on a late night book program when I got my big crush. He had written poetry and was an intellectual, both of which impressed me. My mother found out he was a bachelor, although she warned me that the age difference might be an impediment, as he was in his mid-thirties. The whole thing was hopeless, but she was undaunted.

"You can get his interest," she said, "but you may not be able to keep it."

There was no way we could meet, I thought, but she devised a plan involving her Parisian cousin's husband, the American journalist. Her idea was to say that he had visited Dublin and tried to get in touch with Rory to give him some cigars. So we bought a box in Fox's tobacco shop, and my mother rang up Rory to say they were for him.

He agreed to meet me outside the Royal Hibernian Hotel.

Wearing a new black Dannimac, I handed over the box.

He looked puzzled and quizzed me crossly, glancing down at my hideous stilettos. Being a lawyer, he suspected that the story was fishy, because he didn't even smoke, but he took the cigars anyway. And that was the end of that—or so I thought. I came home deflated but cured forever of passion. Love was not for me: it was too terrifying. My mother didn't agree and went round the house singing "Love, love me do . . ." The Beatles were her latest thing. She had spotted their talent at once while I, a musical moron, couldn't see anything in "Yeah, yeah, yeah."

A month or so later Rory was having tea in the Shelbourne, where I pointed him out to my mother, as we came out of the Ladies. This time he was across a crowded room.

"Go and talk to him!" she whispered.

I just stood there.

"You'll regret it for the rest of your life!"

The rest of my life? Maybe I would, but could this feeling of dread be love? And would a man in his thirties in a pin-striped suit even look at a gawky teenager? I had just overheard myself being called "angular" by two drunks in the hotel lobby so had no confidence, although wearing a new turquoise tweed coat. Still, I crossed the lounge to his corner, sick with nerves, and asked his advice about college. "Would Medicine mix with writing?" I asked.

Rory coughed importantly, saying he didn't know my background or ability, but asked me to join him. On that occasion he shared his pot of tea, ordering an extra cup for me. I forget what else we chatted about. After a bit, my mother joined us and he left to play football. But he gave me his number to ring him.

I did, and was invited to tea in the Royal Hibernian a few weeks later. Tea with a writer—it couldn't be happening to me. The world was suddenly lit up and everything was in color. I went to meet Rory, but the nervous feeling came back, as I tried to keep up a conversation about literature. Luckily I'd read a book he liked, Michael Farrell's *Thy Tears Might Cease*, so the time flew.

"You need something to write about," he said as we parted on the hotel steps.

It was good advice, but so far I'd had a boring life, although that was about to change.

Chapter Eighteen

My mother always wanted to start again. "Come to London with me," she said at the end of the summer. We had been living in Kilmacud for about a year and I'd left my job at St. Kevin's, tired out with night duty and old people's suffering.

I argued against London, but she would not be dissuaded. America was mentioned because she hadn't seen her sister for sixteen years, but we couldn't raise the fare. No, it was London and that was that: I could do what I liked. The memory of the previous time she had left us alone with our father gave me butterflies. On that occasion she had returned, unable to live without us. Did she feel the same now that we were growing up? Obviously not, I concluded, or she wouldn't be leaving.

I was torn between staying and going. We might never see her again if she went on her own. Or she might do something rash in London. Her marriage had reached a new low, and she had even consulted Rory about a legal separation from our father: *a mensa et thoro*, which was allowed in Ireland at that time. "Never marry an Irishman," she said more frequently now.

Travel involved money. Everything involved money and we didn't have any, only millions of unpaid bills. But this didn't deter my mother. She was still taking pills, and had got me more clothes. It was more fraud, but she justified her actions to me: she was angry with some of her relations for not looking after her better when she was young. They deserved it. Again I should have stopped her, but it was like sitting on a bomb that was about to go off. She had even refurnished the Kilmacud house on Walpole's tick—as usual, my mother had charmed the manager, so parcels were delivered daily.

As a consequence, "Shelley" looked great. There were Impressionist prints from Combridge's art shop on the walls—also bought with a dud check—and sixties-style patterned drawing room curtains with green linen chair covers, all custom-made. The bedrooms had new chintz curtains and matching bedspreads. How could she think of leaving it all now? After all this trouble?

"Don't tell anyone we're going," she whispered.

My mother was also fleeing a Dublin furrier. An ocelot coat had made her a marked woman, she confided in me. It had helped her to get credit because at the time anyone in a fur coat was considered to be well-off. The coat wasn't her fault. Originally she had only tried it on, but the furrier had insisted that she take it home on approval. But things had changed in our family and, of course, she had got too fond of the coat. Now it was well worn, the shop was suing and she might end up in prison. We had tried to sell the coat secondhand to repay the debt, but without success. Another furrier had ripped the lining, saying it was worth nothing. I didn't know why he did this, but he ended up giving me ten pounds for luck.

I did my best to distract my mother, but she talked nonstop about the trip.

"I need to bring the Monsignor to his senses," she said.

She often said things like this. It was cracked.

"And you need to get away from Rory," was another one of her sayings.

Since I never saw him, this was even more cracked.

"Always play hard to get," she added. "You must have more confidence."

Would Rory even notice if I went to London? I had seen him only once or twice for tea since the Royal Hibernian, although I wrote him silly letters. Love was meant to be a woman's whole existence. "To a man it was a thing apart," my mother said, and it was true. I was definitely a "thing apart" to Rory.

"What'll we live on in London?" I asked.

She pointed to her Mater Hospital badge. "I'm a qualified nurse."

"Will it work there?"

"It did in East Grinstead."

She had had a good job at the Queen Victoria Hospital. She could have got a pension, if she hadn't come back to us and damp Ireland. So the prospects were hopeful for another English job. I had never been abroad, but London was the center of gravity for the Irish in the 1960s. I was excited but fearful of going. It might be our turn to be refugees. I tried to point this out.

"You've no spirit of adventure!" she said.

I could stay in Dublin, if I wanted, she repeated over and over, but God knows what would happen to her then, I thought. I didn't tell my father, because relations were so bad between them. Since I usually took her side, he ignored me too. Freddie was still the only child he seemed to notice. He was always a good father to him.

Aer Lingus had besieged us in our own country with its high airfares which nobody could afford, so there was no question of us flying. We took the 46A bus to Dún Laoghaire and joined the line of emigrants queuing for the mail boat with cardboard suitcases. I carried a leather weekend case from my mother's checkered youth, with unused pockets for posh creams. It would one day be mine, she had promised, for my future travels. I packed my Aran sweater and wore the red Chanel suit with the black pillbox hat. It would never be me, but I wanted to please her.

Her extravagance came from a youth of Cunard voyages back and forth to America, I had decided. Train journeys also brought back dinners at the Captain's table, telegrams, and dancing with handsome young men. Any shabby station café could evoke this exotic past and, in memory of those times, she always ordered bacon and egg with a pot of tea and toast. That time we had a sandwich on the boat, as my mother told me even more stories about her life before and after she met my father. Someday I too would go to America, she promised, although I still favored the African missions. The thought of my noble future consoled me, as we queued for watery tea in paper cups while other passengers vomited on deck.

It was dark at Holyhead. After the rough crossing, with no sleep in unwieldy chairs, I was worn out. We disembarked and followed the other Paddies herded through customs. There were long tables, and inspectors looked through our cases. It was before the Troubles, the recent violence in Northern Ireland, but detectives scanned the crowd. At last we boarded the Euston train and were soon screeching through Wales, fortified by more tea and sandwiches in cellophane packets.

London was next: I knew the names of its streets from Monopoly. It was also part of the setting for John Buchan's *The Thirty-Nine Steps*. Maybe we would find the steps somewhere near Waterloo, or go to 221B Baker Street where Sherlock Holmes had supposedly lived. My mother was keen on the Kennedys, but also a Prince Philip watcher. Because of our old neighbor's books about the little princesses, I wanted to see Buckingham Palace. It was the time of the Profumo affair too, a political and sexual scandal which had intrigued my mother. Everything would be OK, I told myself, as the train tore through the dark countryside. My mother would get a job in London and we would be back in the swing. I, of course, couldn't stay beyond September because of my pending medical studies; I couldn't miss lectures.

At Euston the train clanked to a stop. It was gray and rainy. We followed the case-carrying crowd through barricades, then queued for the Ladies before finding the taxi rank. Red buses had started up, but there was no public transport or seedy bed and breakfast for us. We taxied to the West End. If we had any cash left, this must have used it up, but a taxi was essential—my mother was adamant about that. We zipped through Hyde Park, then Park Lane, stopping outside the Grosvenor House Hotel where liveried doormen rushed for our cases. She had stayed there on her one holiday with my father. "Always stay in the best hotel," she whispered, reliving the experience.

As we waited in the plush lobby, I wondered how we would pay. But there was no room in the inn and the receptionist directed us to the Mount Royal, an overflow hotel near Marble Arch. It was smaller but still the West End, which placated my mother. It had white marble steps, a white marble lobby, and was far too high-class. But it was before credit cards, so they took us in.

The only residents in the dining room that night, we ordered from the à la carte menu: soup and lobster with Muscadet wine. I had never had shellfish, but my mother was an expert on how to eat it. The next morning I hid under the covers, as Room Service delivered breakfast in bed. How were we to pay for it all? My mother told me not to be silly. She would settle the bill with her first salary, and we could then rent a flat. Everything would be fine.

But her sums didn't add up: the nursing agencies had no position for her. I don't know why this was. Perhaps they saw that she was hyper, in the middle of a manic episode. Such things were not talked about then and it had never occurred to me, clever as I was meant to be, that my mother was mentally ill—I realized only later that her rude letters and shopping were also symptoms. Otherwise I would have stopped us going to London: told my father or rung the Monsignor for help.

Olwyn now says I was worse than our mother: I should have known better. Maybe that's true, but, despite knowing that my father had a brain lesion, I knew nothing about bipolar illness. I thought my mother was temperamental and had had a difficult life that made her unstable. I feared that if she went to London by herself, she might never come back.

I should have looked for a job myself, but I was paralyzed. I had worked in St. Kevin's Hospital, so was surely employable now. But we didn't have a proper address and my mother kept saying she was the qualified one, and on "no account" was I getting a menial job. I felt an agony of uncertainty, a searing fear of homelessness. When I did venture out of the hotel room to walk around the shops, I was afraid to leave my mother's side. Marks & Spencer was mesmerizing, with bargains galore, but we had nothing to spend. I watched the buses tearing down Oxford Street, unable to figure out how pedestrians crossed the street. I finally discovered an underpass beside the Cumberland Hotel, having been nearly run over at Marble Arch. Why were the cars going so fast? Dublin cars never did; everyone jaywalked there.

I longed to go home. A home was a basic necessity of life. After years of wandering, we had one of our own, yet I had left it on my mother's whim. Pre-med was meant to be starting in a month. I had swapped courses, so my fees were in credit, since the university had allowed me to defer from Arts to Medicine. I was going back, as soon as we were settled, my mother kept saying. Then I could visit her during the holidays; she was moving the other children over one by one. We were starting a new life. Our father could do what he liked—she was finished with him.

The days passed and my desperation increased. Sick of French food, I dreamt of tea and bread and butter, my favorite things in the world. I hated the porters rushing to open the door as we left the hotel. My mother said they were only doing their job, but I knew it was for a tip. All our money was gone, and we were prisoners of the Mount Royal. I imagined our fate when we were found out. They would call the police or make us wash the dishes. How many would we have to do? I tried to calculate, as the bill got bigger and bigger.

"This is the thanks I get," my mother said, seeing my mood.

"Can we go home?"

"I can't stand people who throw in the towel."

"I'm not. I want to go home!"

"Rory won't miss you then."

How could he, since he didn't know I was gone? I wanted to be in love, but my feelings were merely an obsession. At the time I didn't know the difference between the two. My mother constantly emphasized Rory's "potential," but the notion terrified me. According to her, I was now old enough to be married—she was doing a U-turn in that department. Marriage had always been out, especially marriage to an Irishman, no one like my father anyway. I was beginning to see the holes in her logic and had been a lunatic to come with her. Yet I reminded her in desperation, "You're the stable parent."

"I am. I'll wangle something."

We tried the evening papers, but nothing. No one wanted a night nurse, or any kind of nurse. We were stuck in an alien city, friendless, with no hope of a return ticket. There must have been aid for stranded travelers, but we didn't know about it. My mother was too proud to ring my father, who might have come up with something. I suggested trying the Irish Embassy, or even boarding the Holyhead train illegally. If we gave them our name and address, they mightn't put us off. Dublin bus conductors never made you walk home. If we got onto the Holyhead ferry, they could hardly make us swim.

My mother finally rang my father's niece, married to a rich dentist and living somewhere in the leafy London suburbs. She drove up to meet us, impressed by the West End. I know my father had been generous to her mother in his palmy days. He had helped with this cousin's extravagant wedding in Dún Laoghaire's Royal Marine Hotel about ten years before, when his generous check had been displayed in a cabinet—it was a bizarre custom of the time. Barry had been a satin-suited page, and I had worn a straw bonnet and mauve dress for the occasion. My cousin must now have been in her thirties. I always thought her beautiful, but she looked strained and gray-haired as she came into the hotel room, and even unhappier than we were. She faced us on a hard chair, while I sat up on one bed, and my mother, who had ordered tea from Room Service, on another.

"You'll need a life without stress for your studies," my cousin warned me, her tone hinting at the impossibility of this.

I nodded as she told me she regretted not obtaining a profession herself. Our request for a small loan was refused. Now I see it from her viewpoint, but then it was humiliating. How had I ever agreed to come to London with my mother? I was as mad as she was.

Then we phoned Uncle Jock, another of my father's brothers. He was a prodigal son, cut off with only a shilling in his father's will. The crime was alcoholism. There were other rumors about wild Uncle Jock gambling away fortunes and farms. Anyway, he had been exiled to London like generations of Irish and was now living in a Kilburn flat with his second wife, Auntie Meg, a white-haired Londoner whom everyone looked down on—why, I knew not. When my mother telephoned, Auntie Meg came at once and took us by bus to see my uncle.

Uncle Jock had visited us on summer trips when we lived in Dún Laoghaire, so I knew him vaguely. He was a small man with a red, whiskey-veined face and a boxer's broken nose. He wore a formal three-piece tweed suit and smoked a pipe. I remember his warmth and delight in me, as we chatted in the kitchen over a home-cooked meal. It was so much better than sole bonne femme. He talked for hours about books and gave me a second-hand copy of Zola's *Rome*, which I still keep in his memory.

My mother explained to him that things hadn't worked out as planned, and we wanted to go home. When she nervously requested the return fare, he supplied it immediately, adding the bus fare back to the hotel and a whole fiver for me. I was to see the sights: Buckingham Palace, the Changing of the Guard, the Tower of London. I couldn't come all this way and see nothing, he insisted.

I lost the fiver, I don't remember how. The next day, my mother and I secretly left the hotel, abandoning her leather suitcase with its hopeful pockets and wearing two sets of clothes: I wore my black Aran jumper over the hated red suit. We walked around for a bit, shopping for Mars bars to bring home, and then, to my great relief, caught the night train to Holyhead.

It was another mammoth journey, but we were homeward bound. As fields flashed past, I tried to read Zola. We shared a carriage with a group of male students from Dublin and Galway, returning from vacation work in English factories. To my surprise, they chatted me up, so I put my book aside, whose title had impressed them. One student, also about to start Medicine, became my first boyfriend. In the early days of pre-med, he took me to the Trocadero Restaurant, spending his hard-earned summer cash. It was my first date, and it seemed amazing to enter a world where men paid for you. It was easy to talk to him too, and much better than love. I was right: Rory hadn't even noticed that I'd gone, but I now had something to write about.

Chapter Nineteen

There wasn't much curiosity on our arrival home, so we didn't mention our adventures. The Mount Royal (today called the Thistle, and offering special rates) billed my father, but he probably ignored it—I don't remember. My mother had signed the register, yet he was picked on to pay; in those days a husband was responsible for his wife's debts. But my father, on the advice of his solicitor, had recently put a boxed notice on the back page of *The Irish Times* to declare that he wasn't responsible for any of my mother's debts.

To my mother's generation, newspapers were for births, marriages, and deaths. Having your "name in the paper" in such a way was a public disgrace. I was sorry for her humiliation, but didn't care myself what anyone thought of us. In school, I had learned to ignore snide comments about my parents' "separation" and was above bourgeois sympathy. I had my armor of books and, in a way, enjoyed being different.

I had started pre-med that October, along with Barry. He had earned his fees in St. Kevin's too, working at night on the ambulances. Originally he had aimed for Hotel Management, but couldn't afford it, so registered for Medicine instead. My problems now were physics and chemistry. Since I had hardly any scientific background, except for botany, and had learned nothing from Mr. Templeton, except how to dodge his advances, it was hard to keep up. I deluded myself by believing that because of a certain academic success in school, I would have no trouble now, but that wasn't the case. The lab smelled horrible too, and it finished me when I had to cut up a dead dogfish. Besides, there was the constant problem of finance. Medicine cost more than Arts, and now there were two of us, so I abandoned my dream of the medical missions, returning to First Arts. I could have struggled on but it wasn't for me and although, like everyone, I have regrets in life, I have never had a single one about abandoning Medicine. But I am still interested in the subject, especially in mental health.

Around this time, Aunt Noreen invited me to dinner and we buried the hatchet—somewhat. On my way home, as I sat on the bus between the two houses, president John F. Kennedy was shot. Maurice opened our hall door to me, yelling, "Kennedy's dead! Kennedy's dead!" It was a great shock. The country was plunged into grief. He was the Irish emigrant-made-good, the handsome young president who had faced down Khrushchev and saved the world from nuclear disaster—that's what everyone thought, although it isn't strictly true. At the time, I cried so much that my mother gave me one of her sleeping pills, which knocked me out.

Maurice was now of age, and the remnant of his inheritance was shared between himself and my father when they broke the entail. Most had been eaten up by lawyers, so there wasn't enough to pay my mother's accumulated debts. Running away had solved nothing. The Sword of Damocles fell when she was finally sued by the furrier, plus about half a dozen other shops. I felt guilty for my lack of clothes sense, because she had procured many of them for me. Because she was a nurse, we had a phone, which was unusual at the time, and now the guards rang: she was to go to court in the near future. I didn't know what to do. All looked lost, until Rory came to the rescue.

My mother told him everything and, being a lawyer by profession, he agreed to help. She still believed in luck, or her capacity to charm. She met Rory in a solicitor's office, assuring him that a detective with influence had promised to get her off. He pointed out of the window at one of the men in old railwaymen or bus conductors' hats who, in those days, looked after your car for sixpence. "You see that car park attendant?"

My mother nodded.

"Your detective has about as much influence as he has."

Rory was tough on my mother. She had met her match and had to agree to do everything he said. But would he be able to save her from disgrace? I didn't look forward to visiting Mountjoy Jail. And, according to Rory, it was lucky I wasn't going there myself because I had been her accomplice. I had also worn the ill-gotten goods, so maybe he was right.

With the worry of this, my mother got sick again and was back in the Richmond Hospital, once more under her consultant cousin. Her heart was weak and she had another bleeding ulcer. There was a fierce sister in charge of the bleak hospital ward, an annex with the Dickensian name of Hardwick Top.

One day, seeing my mother's worried mood, I phoned Rory, asking him to tell her that everything would be OK.

"I can't," he said. "Then she won't do as I say."

He was probably right. It was hard to get my mother to do anything. I was the only one of her children who knew how serious things were. I don't know if my father even knew. If he did, he chose to ignore it, spending most of his time in the pub, drinking with a group which Barry told me included the writer Brian O'Nolan, otherwise known as Flann O'Brien, who meant nothing to me then. Or else he was flying to Manchester where he was being interviewed for some sort of sales job. I visited my mother at the Richmond every night after lectures in Earlsfort Terrace, walking down the quays and turning right into Church Street at the Four Courts, then on to the old hospital. I loved this part of Dublin and thought it must be because my father's parents had started life there at the beginning of the century, when they ran a dairy. The streets reeked of history. Because of the hospital visits, I got almost no study done.

Father F. X. Martin, the historian and, later on, the famous Wood Quay crusader, was my mother's friend from her Mater Hospital days. She had nursed him as a boy and had admired his sangfroid when he suffered from an embarrassing boil. Although a handsome man, he was a genuine buddy and not one of her conquests. Things were actually the other way around: in his youth F. X. had a big crush on my mother and had invited her to the pictures. He was a schoolboy then and she didn't want to squash his ego, so she went. Since he was destined for the priesthood, his parents complained to the nuns, accusing her of seducing their son. "For once the nuns took my side," she told me, rolling her eyes to heaven. My mother was four years older than F. X. and was used to dating young doctors or U.S. assistant district attorneys, not schoolboys.

When I went to college, Father Martin had invited me for coffee in the Annex—this was the basement restaurant in Earlsfort Terrace which always smelled of stale chips. He treated me as a young person in need of guidance. He had a habit of saying, "The only way to be normal is to behave normally." I don't know if he thought I was abnormal, but I resented his patriarchal interference. He, in turn, was shocked by my daily visits to the hospital and told my mother to forbid me to come because I needed time to study. That was true. Exams loomed, but I was unprepared. I had never written an essay in college and did not really know how to study. Yet I still read books and walked around college, crossing the crowded main hall by going up one stairs and down the other. I must have had some sort of social phobia to do with crowds, although I made friends in the Ladies' Reading Room where women students left their coats.

Because my mother was in hospital, things seemed to improve between my parents. My mother always kept up with newly published books or anything that was risqué. One day my father, after looking for work in England, came back with Daniel Defoe's novel *Moll Flanders*, which was passed on to me, as the reader in the family, because it was the wrong book. My father had been instructed by my mother to get *Fanny Hill* by John Cleland, written while he was in a debtor's prison and originally published in 1748 as *Memoirs of a Woman of Pleasure*. It had been republished in England as *Fanny Hill* in the wake of the obscenity trial of *Lady Chatterley's Lover*. Since it had been banned for its salacious content, the novel was unavailable when my father inquired. The earlier, more classic *Moll Flanders* was the same genre, so the bookshop assistant had sold him it instead. It was a moment in time, and I can see my parents in that workhouse ward, with us standing round the bed, laughing together like two teenagers about his efforts to get the banned book. Why couldn't they always be like that? They were still in love in a way.

I distracted myself by falling for an arts student. He was a tall handsome boy and ex–British army. But he was going out with someone else and not free, or so I thought. Father Martin had been shocked because this boyfriend had called his mother a bitch—I had told my mother and she had repeated it, a habit of hers. One day in a lecture I noticed a skull and cross bones drawn on his jeans. I touched it playfully and he froze, but told me to do it again. He later went to England and I never heard what became of him. He was one of the "many young men of twenty" who said goodbye.

The night before her court case, my mother was discharged from the Richmond. I don't know why this was, since she was still under medical care, but perhaps the hospital didn't want to be involved in a trial for fraud. I don't know. Anyway, we stayed together in the Clarence Hotel on the quays to be near the Four Courts. I'll never forget that night. We had dinner together like old times and went to bed early. I don't remember who paid, but someone must have. Anyway, everything was above board and we didn't have to sneak out the next morning.

Rory forbade me from attending the court, so I waited in a nearby café. I was worried, but trusted him. He would get my mother off, I was sure. Of all the people in my life, Rory was the only one who helped me at that time. I was young with sole responsibility for a mentally ill mother. Rory put on his lawyer's wig and never expected thanks, or even mentioned it to me again, only said, "Your mother has high nervous tension." Our relations were sick of her: she had gone too far this time, written too many checks and sent them too many snorters, saying she had a gun with three bullets, one for Cousin __, another for __, and another for __. I don't blame them now because they didn't know that her symptoms were consistent with bipolar illness. Life had got too much for my mother and I regret that I didn't do more to stop her wild spending. But how do you stop a hurricane?

After the court case, she appeared in the café . . . on her own.

I asked her how it had gone, nervously expecting some terrible news.

But she smiled happily. "I saw a pair of blue eyes and knew all would be well."

Rory's eyes were blue.

Chapter Twenty

My mother didn't end up in Mountjoy. If she had been working-class, it might have been different. Such were the inequalities of the time. The newspapers were "fixed" too, because in her youth the director of the *Irish Press* group, Vivion de Valera, had been in my mother's circle of friends. He appeared in the middle of her trial and whispered something to a reporter—newspapers cooperated with each other then: we won't report that, if you overlook this. The judge ordered psychiatric treatment and sent my mother to a nursing home run by French nuns in Dungarvan. She told me not to worry, that it would be a great rest. My father drove my mother and myself down, and we met the doctor who was to care for her: a local psychiatrist, living in a lovely Georgian terrace. This man was always kind to me but was exposed in 2011 in an RTÉ documentary as a serial abuser of his young women patients.

The nursing home was in some sort of converted castle. We left my mother in the care of one particular nun, a stern, capable-looking woman. Everything seemed archaic but my mother had her own room; it was dingy but private, so she wasn't too unhappy. I found leaving her dreadful, but my father and I stopped for tea and biscuits in Kilkenny's Coach House on the way home. He loved driving and hotels reminded him of his carefree youth, when he traveled the country with his rich father.

My father drove Olwyn and me back to visit my mother a few times, but we missed her terribly. She was heavily sedated and a prisoner in the little dark room. It was her first of many sessions in a psychiatric hospital, and I don't know why this one had to be so far away. She could have been sent home sooner but, instead, they gave her too many pills, compounding her addiction problems. I suppose it was the thinking of the time. The psychiatrist, although prescribing them heavily, continued to be kind to me. He once told me that another doctor was driving down the next weekend and I should ask for a lift to see my mother. I did and got one.

To cheer ourselves up, Olwyn and I went to late-night movies at the Grafton Cinema, where we saw such films as *Camille* with Greta Garbo on whom I was totally hooked. I remember us walking all the way home on the Stillorgan Road—as the last bus had gone—happy despite everything. I had started reading Yeats' poems and was impressed with his "A Prayer for My Daughter."

She can, though every face should scowl
And every windy quarter howl
Or every bellows burst, be happy still.

At home, we had to cope with our father's drinking again. Rows happened—natural in a small house with too many people. I avoided conflict, but Olwyn had arguments about our mother's being sent away. It angered her: she thought that everything was our father's fault. Why hadn't he paid our mother's debts? One of these arguments escalated. It was during the Easter holidays.

Our father was only violent when he was in drink—which was like throwing petrol on a fire. He had previously been barred from the house by my mother but, on those occasions, he climbed in the window. He didn't beat us, the way some Irish fathers did. In our family, we had never heard the words, "Wait till your father gets home." OK, he fought with my mother, but only when jarred, which wasn't excusable but half-explained it. Nevertheless his drinking frightened us, so when Olwyn was upset, I had to get her away. Our problem was no money and nowhere to go. The London episode had taught me the misery of homelessness, but my sister didn't deserve abuse. We were no longer children.

I was afraid to ring Aunt Noreen, but two school friends, also doing Arts, came to the rescue. They shared a bed-sit on a corner of Leeson Street near St. Stephen's Green. Because both came from the country, they had gone home for the Easter holidays and their flat was now free. I rang one of them to ask if we could borrow it for a few days, explaining that things were difficult at home. The Wicklow friend agreed to let us have the key. So I caught the bus to her house since we didn't have the fare for two. It seemed to take all day, and, as my friend muttered that I must be "wild" to be running away from home, I said nothing. A Sahara of experience separated us. My mother was in a hospital for bouncing checks, while hers made apple tarts. Her father was a dispensary doctor, while mine was drinking himself to death. Her beautiful old home reminded me of Dubber with its ancient trees, now lost forever, along with everything else in our life, but I couldn't give in to despair. I had the key to a new life for my sister and me.

Olwyn was waiting on a bench in the Green. It was spring, so daffodils were everywhere, giving me a feeling of hope. I waved the key. "Got it!"

The bed-sit was a double room on the ground floor of a seedy Georgian house. It had two single beds, cooking facilities, and a bathroom in the hall. This was proper student life: freedom from parents and peace to read and study, something I felt I'd never had. The only problem was no food, but we must have managed somehow. Maybe we ate what my friends had in the cupboard or perhaps we scraped up some money: I don't remember. As soon as the weekend was over, I would return to my job at St. Kevin's as a nurse attendant. It paid well and they always needed temporary staff. Then we would get our own flat. My sister would go back to school, while I would give up college. I intended to go back later as a night student. Maybe I could contact Aunt Noreen and she would help us to start a new life? But I felt I had let her down, so I didn't.

Since my mother wasn't allowed phone calls, I wrote, telling her my plans and urging her not to worry. I thought she would be proud of me for defending my sister. I wrote to Rory too, explaining all, then rang Father Martin from the coin box in the hall. He asked for my number, ringing me back immediately in case we were cut off. This was considerate, but, to my surprise, he said I was acting illegally. "The law considers you an infant if you're under twenty-one," he said.

I had coped with the adult world since the age of eight and felt far from that. Father Martin went on to say that I could be up for kidnapping my sister. We were to return home at once. There was no reply from Rory or my mother. After a few days, I got a note from the nun in charge of her, ordering me not to write to her again. This was a terrible shock. Why couldn't I contact my own mother and what right had this stranger to tell me off? Only later did I learn the reason.

Nowadays there are stabbings and shootings daily, but there was hardly any violence in the Ireland of that day: it was just gray and depressing. We were a poor, damp island on the edge of Europe. But the year before there had been a notorious crime in the kitchen of a Dublin restaurant, The Green Tureen, just across St. Stephen's Green from our seedy bed-sit. Shan Mohangi, a South African medical student, the last man in Ireland to be sentenced to hang and to be put on death row, had accidentally strangled his sixteen-year-old Irish girlfriend, Hazel Mullen, in a jealous rage. The country was particularly shocked as, in panic, he had tried to dispose of her body by chopping it up, boiling it down, and putting it in bin bags. The smell had been terrible and had given him away. The thought that we were in similar danger must have terrified my mother. She had tried to leave the nursing home and come to us, so was confined against her will. I didn't anticipate this. It hurt me that I had made her suffer.

We had returned home on Father Martin's advice. Also, an apology had come from my father through Evie, our younger sister. My father bought Olwyn a gold watch to make up for his behavior, and that summer he paid for her French language course in the convent where my mother was still confined.

My mother came home at the end of the summer, not cured, in fact worse. It was after this nursing home spell that Olwyn and I realized that our mother had become a serious drinker herself: I met her one afternoon coming out of a pub opposite our house. For the next few months, I went on long walks with her, as far as Churchtown or even farther, in an effort to distract her from alcohol and get her fit again. Walking is the best therapy on earth.

Chapter Twenty-One

My father and I had mellowed towards each other. He had given up saying my mother had poisoned my mind, which wasn't true, and I began to accept him more. I was no longer a teenager and knew how easy failure was. The difference between it and success was the thickness of a piece of paper. Life could go either way for anyone: it was chance, not choice.

My father, only in his mid-fifties, had a weather-beaten drinker's face but was still well groomed in perfectly tailored suits. He probably considered his life a failure—except for his children, in whom, I know, he took great pride. Never expecting to marry, he had fathered six of us. Much of his misfortune was self-induced, but some wasn't, as postwar Irish farmers suffered as a group. And my father had the added difficulties of an entailed inheritance and an unsympathetic family. Loving in his own way, he now spent all his time looking after Freddie, who, although artistic, had learning difficulties at school. My father had always taken an interest in our education, sending us to the best schools, and recently he had arranged, through Father Martin whose sister was a nun there, for Evie to go to Kylemore Abbey since she too was having trouble fitting in. He was especially proud that Barry was now in First Med. To him, he was already a doctor.

I was studying for the First Arts exam: my second time to sit it. For my twenty-first birthday my father invited me for a drink. I had never been in a pub with him, as I didn't drink; but recently I had broken my pledge. Now he ordered me a glass of Sauterne—with a small whiskey for himself. He still had a great sense of occasion and his way of making you feel special. He had recently brought my mother and me for dinner to the Dolphin Hotel after a winning bet at the Phoenix Park Races. The summer before, when my mother came back from psychiatric care, they had gone to the west of Ireland on holidays, taking Freddie. It was their reconciliation, and my mother told me he said that he had done her a great injustice. I don't know if this meant his love for Auntie Bronwyn or his ignoring her debts. They had brought back presents: a Tara broach for me and a gold bracelet for Olwyn. There were gifts for the others too, but I don't remember what they were.

"I won't need a dot for you," he joked that day in our local pub. It was his old-fashioned term for a dowry. Fathers of his generation thought they had to pay someone to marry their daughters.

I reddened. "Thanks, Daddy, but I'm not getting married."

It was an abrupt thing to say and I later regretted it.

He nodded understandingly. "You'll change your mind."

"I don't think so."

There was an awkward silence.

He broke it. "You'll meet someone . . . . Always remember I'm very proud of you."

I was confused. What did he mean?

He sipped his drink. "Remember your story in the school magazine?"

I had forgotten my first publication in Loreto *Mission Notes*. It had been a ghost story about a dead child coming back to warn a sibling of danger.

"It was a good yarn," he said, looking into his whiskey.

Praise was rare then, as we were all brought up to be humble. Mother Columbanus never thought much of my writing and had recommended the *Sacred Heart Messenger* for any future publication. To me that was the pits. With all my chopping and changing, I had achieved nothing so far in my life. I'd been cleverer when younger and won all those book prizes. What had happened? My brain had been left behind on some far shore and my writing dreams shelved.

That drink was our first and last together. The wine had no effect on me, but my father got tipsy. This puzzled me. He'd had *one* drink. For once I was a witness. How had it affected him like this? His brain "lesion" was at the back of our collective consciousness. We knew it was there, but we still didn't think it serious. It was just something that made him unable to cope and to behave oddly at times.

Shortly afterwards my father and I watched Winston Churchill's funeral on television, which was a moment punctuating life, like Kennedy's death or the Twin Towers attack. We were both interested in history and moved by the end of a great man, carried with pomp and ceremony through London, and by barge to his final resting place in Oxfordshire. It was one of the few occasions I watched television with my father, but I didn't know how ominous it was. After that he became daily more confused. One day in March Olwyn found him in the bathroom, trying to turn off the taps. She called me. He didn't know where he was, so we got him into bed and rang the family doctor, who refused to come. Our father had recently been charged with drunken driving, so the doctor probably thought this was some ruse to avoid prosecution. My mother contacted a friendly guard, telling him her husband was seriously ill and unable for court. He promised to help, but probably could do nothing.

The family doctor also ignored a second call. Again, perhaps he thought my mother was exaggerating the symptoms, in view of the pending driving charge. The parish priest, who lived across the road, also refused to come, probably also suspecting some other ruse. This had a big effect on me for my father had been a faithful Catholic all his life: now he needed a priest, but he was denied the last consolations of the church. We had sacked his solicitor and hired Mr. Greene, a kind man with mutton-chop whiskers, who came out to the house and helped my father make a will. I was named as one of his executors, which touched me greatly. On St. Patrick's Day our father was taken by ambulance to the Richmond Hospital where he was diagnosed with cancer. His hair had turned white and he lay in a cot, staring at his hands like a baby.

The rest of that spring and summer is a blur. A niece of my father's drove us in to see him every day, but he got more and more childish. Early in the morning of the July 10, 1965 we got a phone call: our father had died of a malignant brain tumor. He was only fifty-six.

It was just a phone call. No words of consolation, no counseling. Our family had experienced a tragedy as bad as any in Shakespeare. The only difference—a curtain would not fall at the end of the play. My emotions were frozen and I felt nothing at the funeral, only a sort of hysteria: something must be wrong with me, I thought. I loved my father, but why wasn't I sad? His life was a tragic waste, lost to drink and unfulfilled dreams. Like all lives, it had to be lived forwards, but could only be understood in retrospect. For years he had been sick and we hadn't known. With all the tangles of life, it is often impossible to remember events or what we have felt at a certain age. Writing this memoir has reminded me of the invisible mending done on torn clothes in the dry cleaners of my youth. In some way it has healed me. I also discovered that the overwhelming love of my early childhood was my father. "You were the Queen, and had a special place," Barry recently reminded me. The loss of my father's love was painful but subconscious, and affected my whole life. I wasn't aware that I loved him or of what was to come.

The funeral was in Kilmacud Church, across the road from where we were living. It was crowded with unmet relations and strangers. I realized that, like my mother, our father had had another life—nothing to do with us—as friends from the cattle trade and from various golf clubs turned up. We didn't know any of them. Freddie was only twelve, and I brought him back to the house during the funeral Mass to go to the bathroom. Afterwards the crowd chatted noisily outside the church, shaking hands, glad to see one another. It was an ordinary day to them, but we had lost a father. That's the way life is: as in Auden's poem "Musée des Beaux Arts" about Breughel's

"Icarus": the ploughman sows the seeds, the horse scratches itself heedlessly, while a boy falls unnoticed from the sky.

I was angry at the time. Why was everyone chatting and laughing?

The diggers in Glasnevin Cemetery were on strike, so Uncle Ted employed men to open the grave my mother had bought. It was in the de Valera plot, a special part of the graveyard reserved for patriots—again nothing but the best—and opposite Aunt Noreen's family plot. The newspapers were on strike so we couldn't put in a death notice. I don't know how all those strangers knew where and when to attend. It must have been word of mouth, but Aunt Noreen and her sister were the only relatives who called to the house afterwards, although we had made plenty of sandwiches.

Chapter Twenty-Two

By some miracle, I had passed First Arts while my father was dying. I put it down to my mother's lending me his watch for luck. Afterwards, she gave it to Maurice, which was his right as he was the eldest son. I got my father's scarf, but wearing it didn't console me. Like Dante, I wandered off the path of truth, and woke to find myself in a dark wood.

My mother had organized a summer caravan holiday in Skerries for the family, but that's another blur, although I know I was there because we sang "Summer Holiday" driving down with Barry in my father's Opel. Around this time, Freddie was a winner in the Caltex Children's Art Competition. I brought him to collect the prize and we had our photograph taken together on O'Connell Bridge. I'm wearing an Alice hairband and Freddie's a young boy in short trousers. Later Freddie went to stay with a rich cousin on our father's side, Uncle Ted's daughter. I had never met her, but she had boys the same age as Freddie. I had packed his pajamas, T-shirt, and best gray trousers, also some everyday wear. To me he seemed well-equipped, but the cousin called to collect more clothes, saying he hadn't nearly enough.

That September, I went to Scotland for a week with a college friend and stayed with her uncle, a priest who ran a hostel outside Edinburgh. I lay on the bottom bunk, staring up at the wires from the bed above, talking, talking, talking. I didn't sleep all night, just shared confidences with my friend. The next day we shopped in Edinburgh's Princes Street, looking at heaps of Shetland jumpers, unable to afford any. We went to a bookshop and I bought *The Outsider* by Colin Wilson, but couldn't concentrate on it. Then, having taken a train to Liverpool, we came home by boat to Dublin's North Wall where Barry met us in our father's car, which he now drove full-time. Maurice had inherited everything else, so I wasn't needed as one of the executors.

Back in college for Second Arts, I began to have difficulties sleeping and concentrating, so I went to see the college psychiatrist, Dr. Fahy, on the advice of my friend. He admitted me to St. Michael's Hospital, Dún Laoghaire, for a checkup. There was no definite diagnosis, but he told me that I was depressed. My mother didn't believe him and wanted me out of hospital, and back to normal, coping by her side.

"There's nothing wrong with you!" she said.

I was discharged, but resented her interference. I wanted to grieve for my father, but wasn't allowed, or so I felt.

A month later, not any better, I went to see Dr. Norman Moore, a prominent psychiatrist, at his rooms in Fitzwilliam Square. My mother brought me, so she must have been worried. My emotions about my father were still frozen. I had no appetite and couldn't erase certain intrusive thoughts from my mind—my feet were gone like the character in the story "The Red Shoes." It was some sort of symbolism. The doctor said that like many artistic people, I was obsessive-compulsive: it was like walking on the lines of a pavement but avoiding the in-between slabs. Later in life I was diagnosed with mild Raynaud's disease so, as my feet were always cold, perhaps this was the cause.

"Don't worry, I'll get you better," he said, admitting me to St. Patrick's.

The hospital is on James Street, past the Guinness Brewery in an old part of the city. "Festina Lente" was inscribed over the door and there were different floors assigned to the various levels of illness. It was like the three parts of Dante's *Divine Comedy*: the locked wards were upstairs—that was purgatory; down in the basement, the older, hopeless patients spent their lives in bed—hell; in the middle was the ground floor, with an open door policy for the more hopefuls, which represented heaven. I had a room there. The ground floor wards were mainly for sufferers of depression and consisted of two long, polished corridors with rooms opening off them which met at the reception hall. One side was female, the other male. Because I had been in boarding school, the atmosphere was familiar. It was a cozy enough hospital, with a café and comfortable leather couches, founded by Jonathan Swift for the people of Dublin.

He gave the little wealth he had,
To build a house for fools and mad:
And show'd by one satiric touch,
No nation wanted it so much.

Swift's ghost was meant to haunt the place, and I imagined him padding corridors by night, checking that his wishes were carried out. In those days, you rested at the beginning of your hospital stay. My room was beside the Solarium, a small unit at the end of Ward 5, for females who were confined to bed. I got into conversation with some of them, who seemed perfectly OK to me. Anyone could have ended up there, I decided. There was no such thing as *them* and *us*.

"Have you been here before?" a nurse asked, as she weighed me.

I shook my head. I was seven stone ten, one hundred and eight pounds. Although not anorexic, I was uninterested in food. I was immediately given all sorts of pills. One, Largactyl, made my mouth twitch and wiped me out completely. It made me feel worse, groggy and half-dead. Sometimes I woke at night and was given a horrible drink, which put me back to sleep. Sleep had always been a problem for me, so this was nothing new.

The hospital was well organized, like a comfortable rest home. There was art therapy, which I did when I got dressed after a week or so, occupational therapy, and industrial therapy. In the mornings staff members lectured on different stimulating topics: exogenous and endogenous depression, alcoholism, addiction, cross-addiction—which is an addiction to more than one substance at a time, for example: alcohol and pills. Everyone was assigned a doctor—mine specialized in younger patients and was the psychiatrist attached to Trinity College. He was an artistic man and his lecture was called "Tricks of the Mind," in which he quoted the Walter Mitty story about a man who couldn't face reality. It reminded me of my mother—myself too. I was turning into a character in a Tennessee Williams play, too nervous to talk to people.

But the hospital was stimulating and I made friends. I met some cheerful alcoholics, who were always escaping from upstairs and going into the city for a drink and then being reincarcerated. It was an insight into other people's problems, for a change, not my own. One patient, whom everybody called Mrs. G, was the daughter of an Irish patriot. She was a small theatrical woman, probably in her sixties, who was always upbeat. Sometimes she would go into town and wobble back to the hospital in big funny hats. There were two middle-aged Dublin sisters who didn't drink, but walked around together and seemed to live permanently in the hospital. Another friend was a young Anglo-Irish woman in a wheelchair, who had jumped out of a window before being admitted.

"What do you think is wrong with your daughter?" the doctor asked my mother.

"Have you heard the expression 'a room of your own'?"

He had, and this was probably why I had the private room. Our family was squeezed into a small house, which was hard on everyone's nerves, not just mine; but my mother saw my need for space. I had weekly meetings with my doctor, but, although he was kind, there was no psychotherapy, no analysis of my feelings. I had no idea what was causing the winter in my soul.

What was wrong with me? I wondered if my bad experience with a GP when we lived in Dún Laoghaire had anything to do with it. Being a bit of a hypochondriac, I thought my finger had been broken from a netball game, so my mother had said, "Go and see the doctor." Because she was busy working, she didn't come with me. The doctor said that my finger would mend itself; then he began talking about my previous kidney infection. I was puzzled when he started breathing funnily and touched my breasts. "Hop up on there," he said, pointing to his examining couch. I obeyed and he gave me a pelvic examination, putting his hand into my vagina. I was thirteen and didn't understand what he was doing, as I knew nothing about sex. I thought it was irregular, but never told anyone. I didn't dwell on it, but when I found myself in hospital I imagined that this was the reason, since Freud had said all problems were caused by sexual abuse. But my psychiatrist dismissed this, and now I realize that the term "abuse" applies to an ongoing breach of trust from a relative or friend. When I asked the doctor what was wrong with me, he said I was "disturbed." For a while I thought it must be some serious mental illness. No one ever mentioned my father's death, which was the cause. But nothing was now expected of me, which was a relief.

I was free to read but couldn't concentrate on novels. I remember reading a collection of Robert Graves' poems and coming across "Love Without Hope," which reminded me of my feelings for Rory except the gender roles were reversed.

> *Love without hope, as when the young bird-catcher*
> *Swept off his tall hat to the Squire's own daughter . . .*

My grandfather had married a rich man's daughter. Maybe romance was in my genes?

I went home for Christmas, the first without our father. After dinner, my brothers wanted to watch some program on television, but my mother preferred Elizabeth Taylor in *National Velvet*. In our family the battle lines were strictly drawn: if the men wanted one thing, the women wanted another. I would usually side with my mother. That day the row was getting nowhere.

"I vote for the other film," said Barry. "Elizabeth Taylor's immoral."

My mother reddened angrily. "Why immoral?"

"She married four times."

"So what if she did?"

"She stole Eddie Fisher from Debbie Reynolds."

"What would you know about that?" My mother kept her patience; I kept out of it. But she looked at me for support. "What do you think?

While so-so about Elizabeth Taylor, I quite liked the horses. "It's immoral to seduce people," I said.

My mother looked betrayed. "Well . . . who would have children?"

It was funny in a way: Joyce's Christmas row was over Parnell, but ours was about Elizabeth Taylor. In the end we watched the film, although my brothers groaned all through it. Before the day was out, I got weak and seemed to lose the power of my limbs. Again, I think it was the small, overcrowded house. My mother was disappointed and rang my doctor, who told her to bring me back to hospital.

I was in bed at New Year, when Rory visited, giving me one of his poetry books. I was delighted, although it was embarrassing to be in a nightgown. And the nurse stayed in my room while he was there. At the time it puzzled me. Had he requested this, thinking me some sort of mad woman? Or was it hospital policy? Anyway, my infatuation was fizzling out, along with all my other feelings. I wanted to be made of stone, and never to be in love again. It was a trick of the mind, which led nowhere. I had seen my mother's foolishness. Hamlet said it all to Horatio:

> *Give me that man*
> *That is not passion's slave, and I will wear him*
> *In my heart's core, ay, in my heart of hearts,*
> *As I do thee.*

Since I wasn't improving, my doctor suggested shock therapy.

"They don't know how it works, but it does," he said cheerfully. "You'll have some memory loss, but that'll clear up."

"I'll lose my memory?"

"Perhaps temporarily."

I wanted to forget whatever was troubling me, and get on with my life. But I had seen other patients lying comatose in a recovery ward after such treatments, or being helped hobble back to bed. They looked so awful without their false teeth that shock therapy seemed barbaric. Somehow I linked shocks with losing my teeth, but in the end I was persuaded.

It was dark when the night nurse called me on the morning of the treatment. In my dressing gown, I followed her down the long dim corridor to a little anteroom where I waited with other patients. When my turn came, my heart thumping in terror, I went into the torture chamber full of alarming contraptions. There were earphones on a side table, which must be to electrocute your brain, I thought.

I lay on a trolley and a blonde lady doctor tied my arm with a rubber tube and flicked my vein. "You have good veins, dear."

I saw the needle and panicked.

"It's all right," she said.

I felt a jab and fluid surged in my ears. I was drowning, but instead I fell like Alice and, the next second, opened my eyes in the recovery ward with the other patients. I had a headache and lay stretched on a bed until a nurse came and took me back to my room. My head soon recovered and I seemed to remember everything.

I had only a couple of more shocks on one side of my brain. They were usually administered in different strengths, either on one side or both. Then my treatment was discontinued, at my request. It was meant to have no permanent effects. But it drew a line across my life. Now it was *before* and *after*: I was split in two and still imagined a past self stranded on a far shore. I had to reconnect with that person again.

My mother gave up urging me to leave the hospital. Looking back, she was right about my going there in the first place. It was a mistake and should have been avoided. But at the time it was considered a remedy for grieving adolescence. I was Hamlette, mourning a dead father and stuck in a rut, unable to move forward.

I continued with art therapy, painting mainly flowers. A study of snow-drops was sold at a fund-raising exhibition. I also did a copy of the Egyptian King Tutankhamun, for another patient, who paid me a pound for it. It seemed a fortune. Maybe I could earn money as an artist? One day an RTÉ crew made a documentary on the hospital. They saw me painting in the art room and interviewed me. I said that life was a series of bridges like my picture, and one day I'd sail under one. I invented it all on the spur of the moment, but it was included in the final film and shown on RTÉ. I was a mini-celebrity and my doctor said my observation was good. After this he arranged for an intelligence test with a Trinity psychologist. When I had to make up stories about inkblots and do a word association test, I worried about not being able to think of anything, but it went OK.

"Mother," the tester said.

"Love," I said.

"Depression."

"Bread-pudding."

My doctor said I had done well, especially verbally.

While I was in hospital, the IRA celebrated the fiftieth anniversary of 1916 by blowing up Nelson's Pillar, which had always been such a handy meeting place. What could be more insane than that? No one in the hospital would have done such a thing. Then one of the alcoholics, with a daughter my age, committed suicide. I couldn't imagine it and sat on the couch, feeling miserable about deserting my own mother. She had once foolishly put her head in a gas oven, but I had pulled her out. She was upset about something that day and being melodramatic, but what if she did it again while I was away? I should go home, but didn't feel able. Then Mrs. G sauntered along the corridor in one of her big hats. I asked her if the patient's suicide might have been an accident.

She sat down beside me. "Don't fret, pet. I'm sure it was."

"How will her daughter manage?"

Mrs. G sighed. "We have to carry on till the end of the road. Come for a coffee!"

"I'm a bit short."

"My treat, pet!"

She led the way to the café, where they had cakes. I've always remembered her cheerfulness in that difficult time of my life. I gave her Rory's collection of poetry when I eventually left the hospital.

As the weather got better, I was allowed out for a walk. One day Rory returned to see me, but I missed his visit. When I got back, the staff nurse took me aside. She was a gruff, motherly woman who had lost part of a little finger. I respected her greatly and felt sympathy for her finger. "That fellow was back," she said casually, dishing out pills from a tray of bottles.

"Oh." I swallowed mine.

"He has no business visiting you."

I didn't like discussing personal things.

"You won't get better till you get rid of him."

I was taken aback. Why did she say that? And so bluntly. She pointed to another patient, a tall, curly-haired young woman of about twenty-nine or thirty, a university lecturer, sitting on the couch with her bearded boyfriend, also a lecturer. "Do you see Susan?"

I nodded. Susan was so far ahead of me in life and achievements that I was in permanent awe. When we first met, she had told me Matthew Arnold was a bore. A bore? How could she say that? I had liked "The Scholar-Gipsy," and said so, but according to her, his only decent poem was "Dover Beach." I hadn't heard of it, so she bought me an expensive hardback collection of his poems.

The staff nurse lowered her voice. "She's been coming back here for years. She'll never be well, because she won't break with that fellow. He's making her sick."

I stared at them, sitting on the couch, two people in love. "How?"

"It's hopeless. He's a married man."

To me they were the epitome of glamour.

She wagged her half-finger. "You can leave here and never look back, *if* you get rid of that fellow." Then she turned to another patient.

Rory wasn't married, but there wasn't any need to get rid of him because I hardly ever saw him. The nurse didn't understand that he was just being kind. The feelings were all on my side. Although I pretended not to believe in love, I still had an obsession. It's hard to know why we fall for one person rather than another. The ball hops where it falls. The wind blows where it listeth. A niece of my father's had said, "He has a look of your Dad." Freud wrote somewhere that we fall in love with our parents and spend our whole lives searching for them in others. There might have been something in that. My father had recently died, but I had lost him years before. It was only catching up with me now.

Every week the patients lined up and Dr. Moore inspected them. It was like the army, and my mouth always went dry with nerves. I wanted to be well, but was afraid to leave the hospital. It was my one dread. How would I cope? How would I ever even talk to anyone again? Thankfully, no one suggested going home for the moment. There was some talk of my visiting Florida, but Auntie Ellen backed out at the last minute. She must have thought I was foaming at the mouth since I was in a mental hospital. It was a pity, because she died a couple of years later and I never met her properly, as an adult.

Aunt Noreen visited me one day. I was glad to see her and felt more of an equal on my own territory, even if it was a hospital. Her son had married and Niamh was in America, studying for a Masters, so now it was just her and her housekeeper. We sat on the couch, chatting in a friendly fashion. The war with my mother had calmed down, as well as Noreen's irritation with me for refusing the commercial course. If I had done it, I would have been making good money by now and could have avoided St. Patrick's. She didn't say it, but I knew it was on her mind. I couldn't explain how impossible it had been to go against my mother. It was like Elizabeth Bennet's dilemma in *Pride and Prejudice*: her mother wouldn't see her again if she did not marry Mr. Collins, and her father wouldn't see her again if she did.

I changed my mind about typing and started a course at Miss Littledale's Grafton Street Academy, paid for by Aunt Noreen, who came to the rescue yet again. I was allowed out daily and walked down Thomas Street to town, smelling the hops brewing in Guinness' brewery. The typing academy was like something out of Dickens, with ancient teachers—at least they seemed so to me at the time. I banged all day on a big black Remington but made little progress. After weeks my speed was no more than five words a minute when it should have been twenty-five. But it was a start on a skill I would need if I were ever to be a writer, although lately I had abandoned that ambition. When I finished the course, the school sold me the Remington for two pounds and I had it for years until it got lost in some house move.

I enjoyed Dublin that summer. When the typing class was over, I would wander into Stephen's Green and look at the ducks, or sit in a deck chair—you could rent one for sixpence then—and admire the flowers. If I saw anyone from college, I avoided them. One day I bumped into a friend called Derek, who asked when I would be returning because everyone missed me. I'm sure no one had, but I have never forgotten his kindness. Youth is a lonely time, when you think you will never find love.

I was bereaved, yet I was treated as if I had some major mental illness. It taints you when you have been in a psychiatric hospital. No one warned me about the stigma and for years I was afraid to tell anyone in case they thought I *was* mad. I wasn't but still thought I would implode if I didn't take the prescribed pills. I needed time to recover from my father's death and, more so, his life. In a way I got that time, with a room to myself for almost nine months. It would not happen today.

Chapter Twenty-Three

In August I was discharged, with nowhere to go. I was forbidden to live at home again or to see my mother, which struck me as bizarre. But my mother agreed and found me digs in Dublin. I shared a room in a house with a gang of country girls, where I waited to return to college. But I didn't fit in with the girls and got strep throat; I was put on antibiotics. I didn't improve and in the end my mother rang Aunt Noreen who allowed me to stay with her on the Howth Road. It was capitulation on both sides.

"Only for a while," Aunt Noreen said. "It'll be up to Niamh to decide whether you can stay when she returns from America."

That was perfectly fair. It was Niamh's home.

With my own room and Aunt Noreen's kindness, my throat got better. I was living in luxury with time and space to read. In return, I helped with the gardening and painted a big hen sign for the gate, because Aunt Noreen sold fresh eggs to the neighbors and passersby. I got summer work as a waitress in Howth's Abbey Tavern. I was paid one pound a night, plus tips and a late-night taxi home—it seemed a fortune then. Coachloads of North American tourists would descend on the restaurant, demanding ice with their drinks, although there was only a household-sized fridge and no proper freezer. They would often order *Blue Nun* wine or another German Riesling along with scampi or other seafood dishes. The ballads were rousing. "Four Green Fields" would rock the rafters and get everyone singing, and I began to feel patriotic for the first time. It was just before the Troubles, so such songs weren't considered to be inciting violence. Even though I got home late, Aunt Noreen couldn't sleep until I knocked on her bedroom door to say goodnight. Niamh finally came home and agreed to my staying on. We had always been fond of each other but now were friends too. She had studied psychotherapy and tried to sort out my problems by talking to me nightly into the small hours.

For Christmas I got a job in Roche's Stores, selling aprons. Later on in the summer, I was a cinema usherette in the Savoy, but I left after a couple of weeks, by which time I had seen *Meet Whiplash Willie* dozens of times. The air was stale, but my salvation was a short documentary film about whitewater canoeing. I imagined breathing lovely fresh air and taking up that sport some day. The documentary was one of the marvelous short films that were always shown in cinemas of the time but now have died out. The Savoy reeked of cigarette smoke, popcorn, and, most of all, fantasy. Again, the line between normal and abnormal was thin. I got friendly with one usherette who believed film stars like Peter O'Toole and Omar Sharif were in the audience—no doubt it was the constant dark. Later on I heard that Omar Sharif did come to Dublin, so maybe he did visit the Savoy, but it seemed unlikely at the time.

After work one day, a car knocked me off my bike when I was momentarily blinded by the sunlight.

"You're lucky," the driver said.

I was puzzled, painfully rubbing my knee. "How am I lucky?"

"The guards didn't see you."

I had been cycling the wrong way up O'Connell Street.

Everyone in the Savoy was surprised when I said I was leaving. Most of the staff had spent their lives there and were grateful for the lowly paid job. To escape, I had to make up a story that I was going mad. Psychiatric problems were even more taboo then and I was allowed to leave without giving notice.

A nervous breakdown is a loss of confidence. In her famous novel, Sylvia Plath described it as like being in a bell jar. A zombie helmet was around my head too: everything was a fog. I wanted to get through it and find a clear space. Being in hospital hadn't done me any good. If anything, I was sadder when I came out although, weirdly, my asthma had vanished.

I still felt split in two and wanted to connect with the person I was before my father's death: the person who read books and wanted to be a writer. But what if that ambition had been the cause of all my problems, was my delusion of grandeur, like my mother's compulsive shopping or falling in love? In future, I was determined to stop talking about writing and be someone ordinary. I would never give "to airy nothing a local habitation and a name" but go down another road and be a teacher. That way I could read books, even if I couldn't write one.

Thanks to Maurice's help with pocket money, I had returned to Second Arts, doing English, history, and ethics/politics. I had to give up Latin because of my own stupidity. I hadn't studied hard enough so my marks were too low to continue with Virgil and the Latin poets. Ethics/politics, my only option, would be boring, I feared, with lecture halls black with clerics. But philosophy turned out to be the subject that gave me the most stimulation. I discovered that all the problems we have today were discussed by the ancient Greeks. The lecturers, both religious and secular, stretched my mind and gave me a social conscience and an interest in politics. Best of all, in the discussion of human freedom, I was introduced to Existentialism. This philosophy said that we were *not* born in chains, but free. It was our choice to be what we wanted to be.

The 1960s hadn't really hit Ireland, but protest was in the air. Students demonstrated against poor housing and marched for those families and individuals who had been evicted. In support of an imprisoned squatter, I sat down outside Mountjoy Jail, until the guards descended. If I were arrested, I realized, it would upset Aunt Noreen. Though in her youth she was a member of Cumann na mBan, a revolutionary group of Irish republican women, she was now a conservative. I couldn't risk it, so I picked up my bed and walked. After all, she had taken me in when I'd had no place to live. Years later she said that if she'd known I'd been a member of the Labour Party, which I was, she wouldn't have let me stay with her. I don't think she meant this, but she described herself as "a *have* afraid of the *have-nots*." Aunt Noreen was a very honest person, without delusions about herself or others. When I said once that she had nursed in Paris and done things with her life, she answered that she had always had her father's money.

On Sundays I took up hill-walking with the banned mountaineering club, buying a pair of boots secondhand. The official club had been closed down because there had been a bad accident when I was in school: two young people had been killed. It was a dangerous occupation, but enjoyable: I climbed Lugnaquilla, a mountain in Wicklow, one Sunday with a group and almost got lost coming down. I joined the Students Christian Movement and got involved in student politics. For a while, I sold *The Irish Student*, a Maoist weekly, outside the university. My first appearance in prose print was a report of a student meeting at which James Dillon, the Fine Gael leader, gave a talk. I popped it into a letterbox in Trinity College, forgetting to sign my name. I was thrilled to see my piece, "Old Radical Gasps," in the next edition of the paper. My first effort at journalism had been accepted. Maybe I'd have a career on a newspaper?

But my mind was still in a fog about my studies. An English lecturer in charge of tutorials had said he would help me when I got out of hospital. He assigned me an essay on Swift, which I wrote and handed in. I got it back with a red line through every page and no explanation of what was wrong. But for history, I was lucky to have had lectures from Denis Bethel, a burly English public-school type who was to die young. He had a brilliant mind, but no pretensions. He took students on Sunday hikes in and around Glendalough and once, when I spoke of my difficulties ploughing through tomes in the library, he told me I would easily pass and to get a child's guide to world history. It was good advice. Up to this, I would borrow a book on, say, the

Reformation, and spend weeks on it. I had no idea how to write an essay, so I copied out points from books and tried to string them together. One tutor said I had too many "purple passages." My idea of good writing was to use as many adjectives as possible. I had forgotten the advice of Mother Columbanus, my English teacher in Rathfarnham: "Good prose is like limpid water; you can see right through it to the meaning."

By some miracle, I passed Second Arts. I was one of the few to pass history, considered to be a hard subject. I think I was just relaxed: I had nothing to lose. Before the exam, Aunt Noreen told me about some French king who played cards before going into battle. So I wrote an essay on him—today I have forgotten which king he was. I passed both English and ethics/politics too. In those days, Second Arts wasn't compulsory and many students didn't sit the exam.

Despite the doctor's orders, I visited my mother at home about once a week. Occasionally there would be flare-ups, when she imagined I had betrayed her by living with Aunt Noreen. Even though it had been her idea, she would sometimes try to discredit me—write a hurtful letter or ring Aunt Noreen up and say I had said things which I hadn't, so that I might be thrown out. Then I would have to live at home again. Aunt Noreen never believed her, but it was embarrassing.

I was furious with my mother. "Just tell me what's wrong with you!"

She didn't reply.

"If I could wave a magic wand—give you anything—what would it be?"

"I'd be young again . . . the most important person in the world to you."

"You are! You'll always be!"

"I hate getting old."

"You're not *old*! But you can't be young again. No one can. You have to grow up like everyone else."

When I said that, however, I realized that my father had never grown up either. What troubled me most was the waste of his life, rather than his death. I was also angry at my mother for involving me in their battles and for insisting that I always take her side, which I did without hesitation. My mother, still in her late forties, mourned his death as if he'd been the best husband in the world. She had started drinking heavily, which puzzled me. Was she an alcoholic too? All along, had she been as fond of drink as he was? We had all suffered because of his alcoholism; now she was doing the same thing. She had always claimed that she drank with our father to keep him safe, but there must have been something more to it. I've read that there's no such thing as an inherited alcoholic gene. If you drink enough, you'll become dependent. It's now known that alcoholism masks bipolar disorder, so perhaps this was the cause. My mother was still addicted to pills—uppers and downers—and didn't seem able to stick to what had been prescribed. Added to all this, she had developed high blood pressure which affected her heart.

That summer Aunt Noreen and Niamh went to Kilkee on holiday. I had a summer job at the time, but in the autumn Aunt Noreen took me to Paris. It was exciting to go to the continent for the first time. We flew with Aer Lingus and shared a hotel room. Our double-bed had one of those vibrating mattresses. I loved everything about Paris: the coffee, the croissants, the museums, and the bus ride to Versailles. The city of love was so different, so elegant, that I vowed to spend my life there, living in a garret and meeting artists and writers, but of course I haven't done so.

By my third year at university, I was getting the hang of history essays, thanks to my tutor, Alma Collins, a school textbook writer. My English tutor was an American professor, Bob Hogan, and somehow I knew that he was an important scholar. His book on Irish dramatists might have been mentioned in *Hibernia*, the fortnightly literary review. Anyway, it was unknown for pass English students to have someone of his standing—only honors groups got any attention from the department. Third Arts general were the dregs of existence, the scrapings of the barrel. But little did I know the future or how Bob would later come into my life. At the first tutorial he talked about the plain style, about which he had written a book. He mentioned Ernest Hemingway and T. H. White, whom I confused with the Australian writer, Patrick White.

"Don't come back until you've read T. H. White," he said to me.

I never went back. I wasn't particularly upset by his remark, but I never got around to reading the recommended writer. Also the tutorials were optional, and I was too stupid to realize that, although he was talking about writers not on our curriculum, he was a brilliant critic. Still, Bob made an impression, and I imagined the big American car parked outside Earlsfort Terrace to be his. I knew he was married with a big family, but somehow his wit and dark good looks remained in my mind. Also his outspoken, jokey manner.

I had another bout with depression in Third Arts. Grief came in big black waves, drowning me. If I rang home, I would start crying on the phone, depressing everyone. I also feared failure at the upcoming exams. I was determined never to go back to St. Patrick's, but I was still taking prescribed medication and attending the Outpatients. One day I decided to have a good night's sleep. If I slept soundly enough, I reasoned, I would feel better, so I took a double dose of pills. I rang my mother to say that everything was OK now, but collapsed in mid-conversation on Aunt Noreen's stairs. Barry, then a third-year medical student, rode over on his scooter. He shouted into my ear, asking me what I had taken.

"The lot!" I yelled back, through the curtain of sleep.

It was seen as an attempt to kill myself.

"You're lucky not to wake up with a guard at your bed," Aunt Noreen fumed the next morning.

I didn't know suicide was a crime and, anyway, I hadn't tried to take my own life. The next day I was brought back to St. Patrick's Outpatients. The doctor on duty was more understanding; he believed my version of events, but gave me even more pills. I didn't know it then, but you need a passion to get through life, not pills. Years later, when I went back to see Dr. Moore, the head doctor, he told me I wouldn't be happy until I had developed my talents. I was an artist. I had to find a way to be creative.

Chapter Twenty-Four

Despite my fear of failure, I sat my final exams. 1968 was the year of the Gentle Revolution, when student radicals took over the university's Great Hall. Change was in the air, and female students had "liberated" themselves a few years before by wearing trousers in the library—it seems amazing now that we were all so tame, but feminism was still in embryo. Denis Donoghue, the distinguished literary critic, had modernized the English syllabus. We now had to write an essay and a practical criticism of a single poem which we hadn't seen before and which counted for a high percentage of our marks. For the final exam we got Blake's "The Poison Tree." The essay question was "Literature is life in parenthesis. Discuss." Gus Martin, a sympathetic English lecturer, came into the exam hall and, seeing me looking puzzled, said, "Do the rise of the novel on that."

We had studied the novel. I had read Defoe and Fielding and absolutely loved their books. Yet I didn't understand the question about life in parenthesis. What could I possibly write? I might be able to come up with something now that I have written novels. I could say that fiction imitates life but is not life: one has a plot, the other is random and episodic. But that day I wrote rubbish. I didn't do well in history either, hungover from no sleep the night before. Still, crazily, I'd hoped to pass.

Olwyn and I went to London that summer. Always the best of friends, we had organized chambermaid jobs in the Cumberland Hotel near Marble Arch. It was a return to the West End for me, the same area where I had gone with my mother on that mad jaunt a few summers before, but it would be different this time. I knew about the pedestrian underpasses now, and how to negotiate the Underground. And, most of all, we had live-in jobs to go to. But on arrival the hotel could employ only one of us. We didn't want to separate, so we declined the offer and stayed a night in a student hostel, sharing the bottom half of a bunk, head-to-toe. As the elder sister, I felt responsible. The next day we started job hunting, but by the end of the day had found nothing. I remember a panicky feeling in Paddington Station as I rang Aunt Noreen's son, who was now living in Maidenhead with his family. He put us up for a night, and the next day we returned to the city and got jobs in the Dominion Hotel at Lancaster Gate, part of the same chain as Dublin's Royal Hibernian.

London was Mecca. "When a man is tired of London, he is tired of life," Dr. Johnson wrote. But we saw the other side of it that summer. The slave labor in the Dominion has given me a lifelong sympathy with chambermaids and hotel workers. We slept in a converted bathroom and were called at dawn to bring early morning tea to the guests. Then we reported to the housekeeper's office for dusters, buckets, mops, and a vacuum cleaner. We worked for a couple of hours before being allowed breakfast. This was cooked by Jennifer, a gay, Basil Fawlty–type male chef, who hated the female staff. "Here you are, ducky," he would say, flinging fried eggs onto a plate and almost throwing it at us.

After breakfast we went back to work, cleaning, vacuuming, and changing the sheets in several floors of bedrooms. Then, after a break of a few hours, we returned again in the afternoon to turn down all the beds. We often walked in on guests in embarrassing positions and were shouted at—all for six pounds a week and our keep. After a few weeks, we decided to leave, because we needed to earn more money.

I saw an ad in one of the tabloids: Two attractive barmaids wanted for Thameside pub—The Anchor, Bankside. Southwark. SE1. £12 pw with full board.

There was also a telephone number, so I rang for an interview. I took the train alone to Bankside—we couldn't afford the fare for two. The pub's second-in-command, a middle-aged man who reminded me of my father, wanted us to start immediately. He was most casual about not interviewing Olwyn, wanting to confirm only that she was not a minor. "So long as everyone's over eighteen," he muttered, rolling a barrel of draft beer to one of the many bars.

The problem now was how to get paid if we left the Dominion without giving notice. The snobby head housekeeper was off for the weekend and was replaced by a pleasanter Spanish assistant. I knew there were strict rules in Spain about girls working, so I spun a yarn that our father, objecting to our having taken such menial jobs, had sent our elder brother to escort us home. He was arriving the next day. The housekeeper was sympathetic to two poor Irish girls persecuted by a tyrannical parent, and she agreed to let us go without notice. I had previously run into Denis, a timid college friend, now a temporary rubbish sweeper on the Bayswater Road, and asked if he would pretend to be the brother. He agreed, and came to the hotel the next day, sitting nervously in the lobby until we got our cards and pay.

The Anchor pub was great fun. We were given digs in a nearby house and got our main meal at the pub's restaurant. It's still there today, at Southwark Bridge, with a deck out over the mighty Thames. The place reeked of history: an inn had been on the same site in Shakespeare's day and the Globe Theatre had been nearby. Samuel Pepys had watched the Fire of London from the inn, while Dr. Johnson had been a patron and a friend of the owner. Nowadays it catered to tourists as well as locals. Every lunchtime, city stockbrokers in bowler hats descended on the small ale bar, which filled up with local drinkers at night. The staff were from all classes and there were two other girl students, from English universities—to us the essence of glamour. One became a costume designer and afterwards I was to see her name on BBC television programs. It was a big, happy family, with a married couple as the main managers who served a staff Sunday lunch of roast lamb and ratatouille.

But there was the nagging worry of home. Was our mother drinking? If so, how much? Olwyn and I felt a mixture of betrayal and delight in our new freedom. We actually discussed staying in London and forsaking responsibilities, but that was fantasy. Our father was gone now, but all the family's problems had morphed into our mother's alcoholism.

At the end of July, I got my exam results: I had failed two subjects, but had to repeat all three. I don't know why I was surprised, but I was. I had failed, failed, failed. It was the story of my life. Yet Olwyn encouraged me, saying that one day I would make something of myself. We gave notice at the Anchor and went for a final shopping spree, buying a load of towels in Marks & Spencer that we kept for decades. Then we went to a movie in Leicester Square—*The Dark at the Top of the Stairs* with Audrey Hepburn as a blind woman. The next day we flew home on a rackety student flight.

Back at Aunt Noreen's, I started studying for the repeats, taking grinds that she had suggested and generously paid for. For the August weekend I took time off, going to Achill with Niamh and her friends. My illusions about camping were dampened at last: I got lost in the dark, couldn't find the tent, and ended up spending a night on the beach. It was freezing, but I tried not to panic. Dawn finally broke.

I sat my exams in September. The English paper had Donne's "Death Be Not Proud" on which we were to write a practical criticism. I recognized it as a metaphysical poem because a friend had given me a grind on John Donne, and I felt qualified to write on it because of my father's death. I still planned to be a teacher and had given up all dreams of writing anything myself. I could achieve sanity only by having ordinary ambitions. So with more help from Aunt Noreen who knew someone in the local technical school, I arranged teaching hours there and planned to do a Diploma in Education at night, starting the next October. "Push and pull" was written on every public house door in the Ireland of the day but applied to all aspects of life then. I'd got my job through influence, but it was dependent on my passing the exam.

While waiting for my results, I was allowed to teach English in Killester Tech. The degree results were posted during class time, so I couldn't go into the university to check them. Aunt Noreen took a phone message from my brother and arrived, breathless, outside my classroom door to tell me the news. I can still see her through the glass, her blue eyes lit up, her tanned weather-beaten face smiling, and an orange scarf tied pirate-like around her short white hair—she had been gardening.

She mouthed the words, "You passed."

I owed her so much. She had rescued me many times in my life, put me up all through college, and understood my mother's unbalanced moods. We were real friends at last.

Chapter Twenty-Five

I enjoyed my year of student teaching, while attending the university lectures for the Higher Diploma in Education. I had made friends with another staff member in Killester Tech and was earning money at last, working fifteen hours a week. The vocational school was for boys and, although there was no corporal punishment, they behaved well. When my teaching was inspected, I passed the practical, thanks to their cooperation.

In June 1969, I went to America for the summer. Because of our split family, we didn't know our American cousins, except for Lillian, which was a great loss. Auntie Ellen had had six children, and Uncle Stephen two, and I was consumed with curiosity about them. So when my aunt's daughter, Una, invited me for a visit, I was thrilled: America was our hinterland, our mother's back story, and Florida, with its beaches and sun hats, seemed like a slice of paradise. Una lived there too, but we were to meet in Las Vegas where Uncle Stephen's son, Steve, was putting us up. Then we were to make our fortunes as waitresses in the Desert Inn.

Las Vegas for God's sake, it seemed like a dream. But I had been pen pals with Una since childhood, so I felt we knew each other well. The truth is: I was better at writing than talking—I had a pen-pal male friend in Kenya and the relationship had grown through letters. But what if Una didn't like me? She had already driven out west, and I was to fly to New York and catch a Greyhound bus from there. It was my grand tour: it's well known that you aren't properly adult until you have traveled abroad. Aunt Noreen believed in independence too, but she worried about my lack of street-smarts. "You'll be mugged in New York," she said. "Or you'll be raped in one of those bus stations." In Paris a few years before, I had been relieved of my wallet, confirming her worst theories, but nothing would stop me now. At the end of the summer Una and I were to drive back cross-country to Florida. "Well, don't write home for money," Aunt Noreen finally warned me.

My mother, not me, should have been going to America, but she had a fear of looking backwards; for her, certain things were too painful. Her brother was in a veteran's hospital and Auntie Ellen had died a few months before. The sisters had not seen each other since 1947, although they had phoned each other and tissue-thin air letters had come occasionally. Now my mother's only request was a box of Russell Stover candy, a reminder of her girlhood. She had never given up her U.S. citizenship and had always kept in touch by listening to Alistair Cooke's "Letter from America" on the radio. We were getting on well again, although I still only visited home. The doctor continued to say that I wasn't to live there and Aunt Noreen enforced this, saying I couldn't stay with her if I didn't obey his orders. But I didn't feel good about abandoning my sisters. I left everything to them, which wasn't fair.

I got a J-1 visa and talked a bank manager into lending me the air fare. Aunt Noreen, who believed a doctor's word was law, insisted that I get enough pills to last the summer. I was still on antidepressants and tranquilizers and took Mandrax to sleep. I later learned that the Mandrax was enough to have me arrested as the pills, called quaaludes in America, were then sold by dealers as recreational drugs. But my supply went undetected through U.S. customs and, on arrival in New York, I took an orientation course in the hotel with the other Irish students. I had a déjà vu feeling: the yellow cabs were familiar from the TV serial *Kojak*, and it seemed I had been in the city before. My grandparents had lived there, early in the century, so perhaps the memory was in my DNA?

My Greyhound ticket was good for a month. I got to Port Authority, New York's main bus station, and mailed a postcard to Una, looking around nervously for muggers. We had been brainwashed in the hotel that the place was full of white slave traders, waiting to kidnap greenhorns like us. "You a hippie?" a man asked me, as I waited in line. "No," I said. Did I look like one? I was wearing my first pair of Levi's, and my hair was short and tidy. But it was the era of hippies and Vietnam; the war was in the air and on everyone's lips. Although we had protested in college, it was a distant thing at the other side of the world and we didn't really know anything about the conflict, or at least I didn't. It was different for young Americans. Una's army husband had recently been killed in an air crash at the base. I used to study their wedding picture, which depicted two happy people. Marriage equaled adulthood and independence, states as yet unreached by me. It was sad to be a widow so young and, with her mother recently dead, Una was doubly bereaved, which was one of my reasons for traveling all that way to see her.

The bus was to take five days to cross the country. As it pulled out of New York and onto the busy interstate, I froze. The man beside me was reading a porn magazine. God, was I safe? The sexual liberation of the 1960s hadn't hit Ireland yet. Television had brought some change, but there was an air of rosary bead repression. Irish writers were still banned, and Edna O'Brien had been denounced from the altar a few years before. But America was obviously a different world. As the bus sped on, Aunt Noreen's prophecy drummed in my ears. *You'll be raped . . . you'll be raped . . . you'll be raped.* I struggled to keep alert: falling asleep would be the end of me. I was sitting beside a sex fiend.

But I awoke in Chicago and the man's seat was empty. As I dashed for the connecting bus, a long-haired blond ran after me. At first I thought it was a girl, but it turned out to be a boy named Peter, an English geology student, "doing" America. We made the bus but, since he also feared preying men, we clung to each other in seedy stations across the endless wheat-filled plains. America was beautiful, as the song said. And big, very big. All the towns looked alike.

We stopped at Des Moines, then Omaha with its wonderful vowels, then Cheyenne, and Salt Lake City. I was living life at last. I had traveled three thousand miles—even if, so far, I had only looked out of the window. The bus was a sort of mobile womb. On the home stretch through the cactus-filled Mojave Desert, reminiscent of so many cowboy films, I started worrying. What if Una hadn't got my postcard? What if she wasn't at the bus station to meet me in Las Vegas?

But Una was waiting, along with my cousin Steve and his sexy fiancée. As the bus stopped and I got off, Una ran over and hugged me.

She was dark and very southern, a bit taller than me and also in Levi's, not widows' weeds. Steve, a Paul Newman look-alike, hovered in the background. He was a snake-hipped dealer at the Desert Inn—not in drugs, but in the game of craps. He had been an army paratrooper, but now wore black drainpipes and a black leather jacket. What Steve made of Peter, I never knew but, because my friend had disembarked with me, he let him stay in his apartment for a few days. As the Irish cousin, I was the object of curiosity.

"What age are y'all?" Steve drawled, looking me over.

"You mean me?" I pointed at my chest.

He nodded, showing no interest in Peter's age. When I told him, he dubiously eyed my wrinkled jeans and unwashed hair. After five days in a bus, I must have looked grotty. Age is emotional, as well as chronological, and although only a year separated us, I felt eons behind him. His fiancée flounced her teased hair, as she click-clicked after him to Una's long blue Cadillac. It was a "used" car, but its vast length impressed us impoverished Europeans.

Peter spent a few days unwinding by the pool. Although standard for a Nevada apartment, it seemed luxurious to us. Everything was. I was to get a job at the Desert Inn, owned by Frank Sinatra of all people. Everything was new to me. Una read Ayn Rand and hummed Dionne Warwick's "Look of

Love." I had never heard of either. Lately my reading was the works of Samuel Richardson, or other eighteenth-century novels like *Tom Jones*. And my taste in music was mainstream—basically Cliff Richard, Simon & Garfunkel, and maybe The Beatles, although they were mostly my mother's favorites. 1960s pop music had almost passed me by. I had never tried marijuana, which my cousins smoked occasionally, but I did in those first days in Las Vegas. It made me sick, proving I was a greenhorn.

"She's not like us," Una whispered on the phone to her sister, when I was in the loo. There was a pause. Then another hoarse whisper, "I dunno—sorta homely."

I flushed the chain: the subject changed. That night I saw myself in the mirror—a skinny, angular body with thick, fair hair. Would I ever fit in, ever be able to get married? Do something more than write letters to people?

The temperature rose to 130 degrees, bearable only indoors where there was air-conditioning. The desert lay beyond the apartment complex, and there was no public transport. There were other difficulties too. To work, I had to join a union, which would cost more than my bank loan. Besides, I was considered some sort of simpleton for paying a newspaper boy ten dollars when Steve didn't get a paper delivery—it was a con trick. So the committee of cousins decided the pace of the Desert Inn kitchens would be too fast for me.

I had served tables all through college but was now told to write home, saying the only jobs in Las Vegas were for topless waitresses—but that the pay would be good for going naked. I just wrote that there were no jobs and I was broke. An American Express check came by return post, accompanied by an angry I-told-you-so letter from Aunt Noreen. I should have taken some action and left Las Vegas, but I was marooned in the glare of the sun, unable to move forwards or backwards. While the others worked, I spent my days by the pool, frying in cocoa butter sunscreen. My only companion, Steve's sexy fiancée, never stopped asking me if she should marry him. I didn't know what to say. He seemed kind and attractive, although macho.

It was the summer of the moon landing. Alone in a darkened apartment, I watched Neil Armstrong take "one small step for man and one giant leap for mankind." It was a miracle, but they stayed up there only for a day. Meanwhile I was on another moon: a place where it never got dark. Everything was so different from Ireland: there was no way of getting anywhere if you didn't have a car. One day I went out, and the cops picked me up for walking on the highway and drove me back to the apartment. It was the same with language differences: people talked about "legit theater." Someone even asked if I spoke English. "We've been speaking it in Ireland since 1169," I said pompously, "although it might've been French or Irish way back then." This brought funny looks. Things came to a head when Una collected contributions for Steve's wedding gift. "We're gettin' a belinda," she whispered confidentially. A belinda? What on earth was that? Now they'd think me really dumb, a definite greenhorn. So, pretending to understand, I handed over my share. It turned out to be a food blender.

Then Steve chose me as his wedding witness—they didn't seem to be called bridesmaids in Las Vegas. I felt honored, but it brought another missive from Aunt Noreen via my mother: I would be excommunicated from the Catholic Church for setting foot in a register office. It was a reserved sin, requiring a bishop's pardon. I ignored this, writing back to my mother and adding chattily that marijuana had had no effect on me. Why was there such a fuss? Beer had more of a kick. This brought angry telegrams insisting that I come home immediately: a case of the pot-calling-the-kettle-black. Our mother/daughter roles were now reversed. She had become the minder and could tell everyone about her wild, drug-abusing daughter.

Steve's friend, a man called Sandy, stored fur coats in the apartment wardrobe. Una and I didn't know if they were stolen or not, and didn't like to ask. Steve told frightening stories of the Mafia breaking dealers' hands for stealing money from the tables. One night we went out on the Las Vegas Strip. Una had fitted me with false eyelashes and puffed out my hair so it was a bouffant style. In skimpy miniskirts, we headed for Caesar's Palace to make our fortunes on the slot machines with all the low rollers. "Isn't this fun?" Una said, as she yanked a machine handle in the dimly lit and crowded lobby. I pulled mine: two oranges and a pear appeared, using up my dollar budget. In other rooms the high rollers noisily played the tables, supervised by slick dealers. Cocktail waitresses flitted around with free drinks. Old men linked half-naked girls. It was the First Circle of Hell, and I burst into tears.

Una gaped. "What's wrong?"

"S-sorry." I couldn't stop crying. She pulled me into a booth and grabbed two whiskey sours from a passing cocktail waitress.

I sipped mine. "I want to go home."

She was flustered. "OK . . . I'll drive you."

"I mean back to Ireland."

"You can't do that!"

A false eyelash fell into my drink. "I hate this place."

She looked at me with disbelief. "But this is Caesar's Palace. We could see movie stars. Vic Damone's here."

I'd never heard of him. "I'm almost out of money."

No one in Las Vegas ate in. "All-you-can-eat king shrimp" had made holes in my meager funds, so now I ordered nothing but pancakes and maple syrup. And my monthly bus ticket had expired. I had expected to earn money for the trip back to New York and my return flight home. How would I get there now?

"I know you're spending money here," Una said reasonably, "but in Florida you'll be a guest."

I should have gone home then and there, but I couldn't leave her, not with all her losses. Looking back I can see that I wasn't assertive, due to my relationship with my mother, who had always taken charge. Also I told myself that if I did leave, the summer would be a failure, after years of correspondence. What would my mother say if I fell out with her niece by leaving early? No, I couldn't spoil everything now. I would wait and get a job in Florida to pay my fare up to New York. We were heading south after Una had visited her former in-laws in Seattle. While she was gone, I was to stay with her younger brother, Tom, in Los Angeles.

Chapter Twenty-Six

I was delighted to get out of Las Vegas. Tom, a big, kind boy, had stolen Una's previous car and driven across country to California, escaping the draft. Now he was a caretaker of a Marina del Rey boatyard where he lived in a trailer with his cat and Bonnie, an unhappy "older" woman of thirty, who had recently lost a baby. The memory often made her cry. I couldn't console her but, despite this, the time was mostly carefree. We ate *in*, to my relief, and spent the days reading and cooking. I was hooked on James Baldwin's novels, while Bonnie made grits and other southern delicacies on the trailer stove. We all got on well, and went to Disneyland three times, which I loved. Those visits were the best thing about my trip to date.

One day the FBI called, but Tom managed to hide. All his friends were on the run from the Vietnam draft. Then Sharon Tate was murdered by the grisly Charles Manson gang. And the next day a man was shot dead right across the street from where we were. I still had troubles with sleep and read Gore Vidal's *Myra Breckenridge* uneasily in bed while the trailer shook as Tom and Bonnie, thinking I was asleep, made love. Although we were living on a fault line, this wasn't an earthquake. I knew the facts of life, but I didn't know lovemaking was so noisy. My only real relationship had been epistolary. I longed for that safety now, writing more letters into the scary night.

Una finally returned. Peter turned up too, just as we left for Florida, and joined us for some of the trip. But he soon departed for the Grand Canyon, because Una refused to make a detour for "more red clay." Trouble with her car didn't help her mood, and my inability to navigate got on her nerves. I wasn't a practical person and there was also the matter of my vanishing funds: she was paying for my pancakes now. But I couldn't write home again: I was already in hock for the rest of my life.

In Aspen, Colorado, we slept outdoors to save money and Una teased me about snakes. With a rope circling my sleeping bag for protection, I studied the night sky. Men had actually walked on the moon. The idea thrilled me and I had a sort of cosmic experience: everything was peaceful and simple. We spent more nights in the car, making our way to Oklahoma where Una's father, a tall handsome southerner, had already hitched up with a new wife. He hadn't seen my mother since the 1930s, but he bought her a dime store bread-basket, explaining that he couldn't afford a proper present. It was penny-pinching, but I still liked him. He told me all about my mother's youth and the hardships of the Great Depression. Una warned me not to mention Chuckie, her Dallas boyfriend, whom we were visiting next. Her father didn't approve of sex outside marriage, except for himself. He didn't approve of many things, especially that Una's late husband had been enlisted and that his eldest daughter Lillian had roomed with a black girlfriend.

Una sang songs by Stephen Foster as we drove. "Way down upon the Swanee River, far, far away . . ." I joined in but had no voice. It took a whole day to get to Dallas. Chuckie, who worked for a helicopter company, was English but looked Texan. He was blond with a crew cut and had a stocky, muscular body. That night we all went out for beer and ballads. I was fixed up with a guy called Jack, but considered anyone over thirty geriatric. Anyway, as an Irish cousin, nothing would be expected of me—or so I thought. The pub was a wonderful night of rousing country music and I sang along, happily downing beer. When we returned to the apartment, I helped bring Una's clothes in from the car. She was sharing Chuckie's big brass bed, so I looked sleepily for the couch. I was saying goodnight to my "date," when she ran out of the bedroom, yelling at me.

I was in shock. "W-What's wrong?"

"You've been making eyes at Chuckie all night!"

"What? . . . I haven't!"

"He wants to sleep with you!"

Chuckie came out of the bedroom and put an arm around me, smiling drunkenly. I pushed him away, turning to Una. "There's some mistake."

But she stormed out, banging the door, and her car disappeared into the night. I was stranded in the middle of America, broke. My "date" shrugged, sighing knowingly as he went to the door. "Have a good time, guys."

Then he was gone too. A "good time"? God, how had I given that impression? What now? I had only seven dollars left and Chuckie was leering again. I had to think of something fast, but I was almost collapsing with tiredness. First I needed a night's sleep. Maybe in the morning I would wire home for more money. "I'm sleeping on the couch," I said nervously.

"Sure," Chuckie drawled, disappearing into the bathroom.

I lay there, hoping he would go into his own bedroom, but he reappeared and stood by the couch, smiling. Something was protruding alarmingly from his dressing gown. I had never seen a naked man, or an erection, and was shocked when he pulled open his gown. Was that to fit inside me? When I turned away, he lay down beside me. I moved to an armchair. He followed, casting admiring glances at his heroic appendage. My cousin had left me with a madman. Trying to keep calm, I went into the bedroom, but he followed me there too. This went on for what seemed like hours—couch to bed, to couch, to armchair, back to bed. Back and forth we went.

"You've ruined everything," I shouted at last. "I've no money to get to New York. Please let me sleep!"

"I'll fly you to New York," he drawled.

The thought made me queasy. "In your helicopter?"

He nodded, blinking. "Just relax. I'll get you there."

"Relax? . . . We've driven all day . . . crossed two states. I have to sleep. You do what you like."

He was getting tired too and hadn't attacked me so far. So I lay down on the big, brass bed, tired beyond caring. You reach that stage sometimes: nothing matters anymore, like admitting under torture to something you didn't do. He got in beside me, but I moved to the farthest edge and lay in a fetal position with my back to him. By now things had deflated somewhat, and he didn't touch me. Unlike a fictional heroine's, my virtue was spared.

I was barely asleep when the door was flung open: Una was back.

She glared at the two of us in bed but said nothing, just grimly went to the wardrobe, unhooked her rails of clothes, and banged back out of the apartment. I lay there, not knowing what to do, as the car started up again. It was the worst moment of my life so far. I hadn't done anything on purpose to upset Una, although she obviously no longer liked me. Now she'd think the worst and would never talk to me again.

Nevertheless, she returned the next morning.

"Hi, I'm back," she said sheepishly.

I was beyond feeling. I'd hardly got any sleep. "Where did you go?"

She gathered the rest of her stuff. "The car-park. Comin'?"

I went with Una. What else could I do? For years I had wanted to meet her and now had blown everything by enjoying the ballads. Somehow I had sent out the wrong message and she would never forgive me. My great adventure had ended in disaster. On the long drive to Florida, I told her that nothing had happened between Chuckie and me. I hadn't tried to steal her boyfriend. I'd never done *it* and wouldn't have known *how*. I tended only to like men who talked about Keats. She nodded, sighing and saying she knew. But she didn't know what I had gone through that night. Aunt Noreen's prediction had almost come true, except Chuckie was a rapist manqué—there was that deflation problem. I discovered there were worse things than hell: a night in Dallas for one. People remember it for President Kennedy, but for me it will always be Chuckie's erection.

We broke the journey to Florida to see Lillian, Una's older sister and friend of my youth, now working for the American Red Cross in Mississippi.

It was August and Hurricane Camille had left a trail of destruction along the Gulf Coast. The Red Cross had set up a refugee centre in Camp Shelby, an army base at Hattiesburg, Mississippi, northeast of New Orleans. Lillian was in charge of recreation. She was still tiny but now a thirty-something. I hadn't seen her for years, so was delighted to catch up. And it was a relief to get out of the car and walk around.

Una and I were volunteer helpers and stayed at the base. I don't remember any adult refugees, although there must have been many. All week I played with the children in a big aircraft hangar, telling them Irish fairy stories and braiding their crinkly hair, supervised by armed, white National Guards, who kept asking if I liked that "kinda work." They meant helping black people. I said I did. I was going to be a teacher and I enjoyed the children's quirky humor.

On the last Saturday night, we drove into Hattiesburg for a hamburger. Five women were in the air-conditioned car. Lillian, Una, and myself, and two other Red Cross volunteers: Alice, who was a black, and Pam, a white Mississippian. After a hard week, Lillian was hungry and wanted to relax. We tried one seedy drive-in after another with no luck. Looking back, we seemed to have been repeatedly ignored, but at the time that didn't occur to us. Perhaps they were just busy, we thought. It was a Saturday night after all.

"Maybe y'all should go back home," Alice said worriedly.

Like all the volunteers, she was in her early twenties. We were staying together, sleeping in bunks, eating army food, but enjoying nightly guitar sessions and singing sixties' songs of liberation: Bob Dylan and Joan Baez.

As we failed to get service in another café, Alice was getting more and more jittery. "Why don't y'all make popcorn? They ain't servin' us!"

"You're imagining things," Pam said. "They can't ignore the law."

"I want a hamburger!" Lillian insisted. Despite her height, she was an emphatic person.

With my diet of pancakes, I had put on a stone. I was looking forward to a hamburger too, with maybe a milkshake and some fries, as the Red Cross was paying: a thank you for all our help. If only we could be served. Finally we pulled into Joe's Place, a rural truck stop at the side of Route 59. Conversation stopped as we found a table in the all-white café. Men in blue overalls whispered to their wives. A middle-aged waiter wiped the formica-topped table and gave us menus and glasses of iced water—all except Alice.

Lillian asked for another menu.

"We don't serve nigger folk, ma'am," the waiter said.

His skin was pitted with acne and he had ugly teeth—unusual for an American. Of all the waiters who have ever served me, his face remains in my memory. We all stared in shock. Alice began to tremble and stood up. Lillian put a restraining hand on her arm. "You're breaking the law!" my cousin said to the man.

His eyes glittered with hatred. “Niggers ain’t welcome here.”

Without a word, we all got up and trooped out into the steamy night. “God bless you and your company,” someone in the café chanted after us. Martin Luther King Jr. had been dead for over a year, and two Civil Rights Bills had been passed. The month before an American had landed on the moon. The voice of Bob Dylan sounded in my head: “How many roads must a man walk down, before you call him a man?”

As we stood outside, inhaling gas fumes mingled with hamburger, the cops screeched up. A brawny sheriff got out of the car, fondling his gun. Lillian ran over to his side, standing level with his waist. “I want to report that café for breaking the law.”

“Ma’am, that’s your problem.”

“But . . . what about the law?” she stammered.

He pulled out his gun. “Move on!”

Although from Florida, Lillian had never experienced discrimination like this, and kept assuring me that it wasn’t common behavior elsewhere in the States. We drove back to the camp in silence. The law had meant nothing. Pam finally apologized to Alice. “That café just made a liar outta me.”

I didn’t think of the incident for nearly forty years. But when Barack Obama was sure of being elected for the first time at about three o’clock on the morning of November 5, 2008, I remembered that night. Then he was elected for a second term. In 1969, it wouldn’t have seemed possible. It shows you can never predict the future.

I’ve read that there are only three subjects to write about: sex, politics, and religion. I covered all three that summer. I also learned an important lesson: not everyone liked me. At the time I felt that the summer had been a failure, but maturity teaches you to see things from another viewpoint. I drove back to Florida with Una and at last visited my aunt’s large home in suburban Jacksonville. She was dead now, but the ashtrays were still full of her lipstick-smeared cigarette butts. I visited her grave that trip, but I never got to see St. Petersburg where my mother had grown up.

My next problem was getting back to New York to catch my flight. The date on my Greyhound ticket had expired after one month. It was written in by hand, so I changed it with a ballpoint to three months. On the day of departure, I went to the Jacksonville bus station, arriving late. As the bus pulled out of the station, Una hailed it down, while I ran to the ticket booth. In her haste, the sales assistant didn’t notice the forged date and stamped my ticket all the way to New York. Necessity knows no law. I was on the first lap home.

I stopped off at New Jersey to stay with another cousin and her family. Her husband brought me up the Statue of Liberty, but I had no funds to see my Uncle Stephen’s daughter in Boston. We did meet many years later in New York and caught up with each other’s lives. Every story has an epilogue and this does too. Despite the Dallas debacle, the past is forgotten and Una and I remained friends. The other day she sent a picture of Tom, with me on the back of his motorbike, clutching him for dear life. We're both carefree and happy. I look skinny, despite my summer of pancakes; Tom was puffy even then. He died of obesity a few years ago, mourned by three ex-wives. Lillian married happily, but died in 2012 of diabetes complications. Even I was to marry, but that was in the future.

Chapter Twenty-Seven

I was back in Ireland, with no intention of ever returning to America. Again little did I know the future. My mother met me at the airport and insisted that I live with her again. Maurice had bought the family a new home close to Ranelagh with his inheritance, and all our furniture had been carefully replicated. With four bedrooms, we had much more space than in Kilmacud. I felt I could now live at home, and Aunt Noreen understood.

But I wasn't at my mother's for long. I had come home late, so the few Irish teaching posts were all filled. Emigration loomed for everyone then. I answered an ad in the *Times Educational Supplement* and got a job in Gordon County, a secondary modern school in Maidenhead, Berkshire, teaching English and history. Maidenhead was one of the few places I knew in England, besides London, because Olwyn and I had stayed there the year before with Aunt Noreen's son. But leaving Ireland was a wrench. Olwyn was finishing a history degree in college and wanted me to stay, but I went in search of myself.

"If you live at home, you'll be back where you started," Niamh warned me as she drove me to the airport. She was now a qualified mental health professional. I still thought I would implode if I forgot to take this or that pill, and another difficult time was ahead of me.

I stayed in a boarding house for my first few days in Maidenhead, then I got a bed-sit in a widow's house with a shared bathroom and kitchen. Maidenhead was a dormitory town in the stockbroker belt, reminiscent of Galsworthy's novels, with Victorian houses and a boathouse on the Thames which hired out motor boats for day trips. I found myself looking for tennis clubs and the Joan Hunter Dunns from John Betjeman's famous poem. The place seemed interesting, but wasn't. I was an outsider and lonely. No one ever spoke to me, and the town shut down every evening, long before the commuters piled out of the London train. I remember thinking that *any* ordinary Irish town would have had interesting characters to talk to, but here there was no one. I was a stranger in a foreign country. The only blessing was the library, which I visited frequently. I found a copy of D. H. Lawrence's letters, which I read for solace in my tiny bed-sit. Solitude became my only friend. There was another young woman in the front room of my digs, and she sometimes invited me in for hot chocolate before bed. I remember telling her that I would marry someone romantic. She looked at me with puzzlement, saying that she wasn't romantic at all. Her husband would be a provider. It was a revelation to me. I had pretended to be unromantic, but wasn't. My mother had had a bigger influence on me than I thought. I had once sat weeping in a dark cinema at the fate of Emma, Lady Hamilton after her lover, Lord Nelson, had been killed at the Battle of Trafalgar. Love was the meaning of life, but would I ever find it?

Originally I had been interviewed for Furze Platt Senior School, the town's better comprehensive, but was offered the post at Gordon County, a secondary modern. It was a Dickensian redbrick building, and the students had a low standard of attainment. My predecessor had fled the job with a nervous breakdown, but I didn't know this. Neither did I know how to teach. Most of the other staff were from English teacher training colleges, which equipped them with practical skills. My diploma in teaching was more academic and had not prepared me for children with such poor reading skills. Some were sixteen-year-old school-leavers who were merely filling in time before taking unskilled factory jobs. They had no interest in anything, so I entertained them by talking about Freud's ideas on the unconscious, and getting them to read any books in the English department cupboard. I remember only one: *White Fang* by Jack London. This worked, but in some of the younger classes there were Pakistani immigrants who spoke no English. My blessing was that they were the best behaved.

The staff lunch, served in the Home Economics kitchen, was worse than any Irish boarding school food, so I found a sandwich shop in the town. There was always a fuss about balancing the pupils' lunch money, which it was my job to collect. One day the headmaster, a nervous case, stood at my desk, his head bent as he counted the money and compared the sum to the cashbook. I was behind him, puzzling over some mistake, when John, a blond boy of about sixteen, crept up and kissed me on the cheek.

I was too shocked to protest. He had obviously been dared, but I knew that the dare would be considered my fault because young teachers never got any support. I'd probably be accused of child sexual abuse. So pretending nothing had happened, I again bent over the cash book. Luckily the headmaster was still studying it and hadn't noticed anything, so there were no repercussions. The culprit usually spent his time sitting in detention outside the head's office, high on Mandrax—the sleeping pill which I had been given legally by St. Patrick's Outpatients.

The school had many children in care who were delivered in a minibus. One red-faced boy, Phil, who was disturbed, regularly sabotaged my classes. Again, any unruliness was considered to be the teacher's fault and previously the headmaster had rushed into my classroom, waving his arms neurotically because of the noise. I didn't want him doing it again, so one day when Phil was acting up, I told him to stand in the corridor.

"No!" he yelled, his tie belligerently askew.

I repeated my request.

He roared at me again, apoplectic. Somehow I lost it. I dragged him to the door, pushed him out, and banged it shut. The class looked at me with new respect. But at the morning break the headmaster ran up to me in a tizzy. "Phil says you kicked him."

"I put him out of the room."

The headmaster wrung his hands worriedly. "This is terrible, terrible."

I looked down at my toeless Dr. Scholl sandals. "If I did kick him, I'm sorry. But it couldn't have hurt. Not in these shoes."

He walked off muttering, "What if the parents find out?"

It was wrong of me to lose my temper, but it was Phil or me. I was learning that teaching is like acting. You have to develop a strict persona or drown.

I had imagined that all the English played cricket, but now I was in soccer country. As the term progressed, some of the school staff befriended me, inviting me over to watch the matches on TV. Although grateful, at the time I had no interest in them. Only years later, when Ireland started winning under Jack Charlton, did I change my mind. I got on well with the art teacher, who was an exhibited painter with long 1960s' hair and a pretty wife. I remember asking him about modern art and what was the point of a painting with one horizontal white line, which I had seen in a gallery. He said that it could have been a beautifully executed white line. Had I ever thought of that? I hadn't. We both hated the school, and during one lunch hour I said I'd never get out of the place. "You will," he said. "You're too interesting to remain here." I didn't believe him, but it was a leg-up to be thought "interesting" for the first time in my life. The gym teacher, a sporty young woman, was pleasant too and always brought in the jobs page of Friday's *Guardian*, which she handed pointedly to me. She advised me to give up teaching—anything would be better, because I wasn't suited to it temperamentally, by which she meant I was too much of an introvert.

I wasn't earning much—sixteen pounds a week after tax—but I had studied hard to get a degree and didn't want to give up everything. I could get on the boat train and go home to Ireland, but that would be failure. Instead I stuck it out, going up to London for the weekends, where I stayed with Evie who was now training to be a nurse at St. George's Hospital in Tooting.

There was a custom for nurses to get free tickets to the West End theaters, so I saw a few plays with her and her friends.

Things improved in the summer term when I shared a flat with another teacher who had got the better job in Furze Platt. Then, one day towards the end of term, my headmaster told me to look around for another job because he wanted to hire someone in Remedial English from a Teacher Training College. I saw an ad in *The Times Educational Supplement* for a residential form teacher in an independent girls' school in Headington, north of Oxford. They wanted a Catholic so I applied and was granted an interview. My headmaster had agreed to write me a reference and the head of history was also willing to sponsor me. To my surprise, he warned me not to use Father F. X. Martin again, who had given me my last reference. I felt betrayed by this revelation. True, I had never been a great student, but strangers, English people I didn't even know, were now doing their best for me. What had my mother's old friend written about me? It was probably to do with my breakdown, which was caused by bereavement. It shows that the stigma of mental illness lives with you.

I was given a day off for the interview. I remember catching the train from Maidenhead to Oxford and walking through the ancient city, entranced with its colleges and dreaming spires. Centuries of learning, I thought, hoping that some of it would rub off on me.

The school was housed in a mock Tudor mansion in its own grounds at the end of a leafy lane. It had been founded by two converts to Catholicism who, while on holiday, had decided to start a boarding and day school for Catholic girls. One of them, the present headmistress, was still alive and ran the school with the help of her sister. They were both Toryish Miss Marples and dressed alike in tweed skirts and twin sets.

I can't remember anything much about the interview except that I was told firmly that the school didn't preach the doctrine of indulgences. Obviously the headmistress thought that since I'd come from Ireland I must believe in all sorts of superstitions such as the medieval teaching that we could buy time off purgatory. Afterwards she brought me into the staff room for afternoon tea. It was full of chintzy chairs and chatty Oxford dons' wives who taught part-time. After a second interview, I got the job. I was replacing a teacher who had an obsession with the Brontës and this was a good talking point.

My time in Oxford was another life. There were ups and downs, but the children were better behaved, and I enjoyed teaching and made friends. It was a happy school, even if I felt overworked. I had a boyfriend, but I won't go into it here because it's another story. One day I went for a walk at lunchtime and lay at the edge of a park, thinking that I'd never be a writer now. I had failed in the main obsession of my life because I didn't know where to begin. Later I spoke to the head of English in the school about my literary dreams. I was hesitant. "Maybe I should try a short story?"

She was married to a university don and emphatic. "No, write a novel!"

I looked at her in disbelief. "Joyce has done everything."

"Nonsense. He brought the novel down an alleyway!"

So my writing bug was reactivated: I could say something too. I didn't have to compare myself with anyone or worry about who went before me. Writing is another case of jumping in the deep end. You do it, then learn by doing.

But, of course, I was too busy to start. A writer is always too busy and invents any excuse not to write. Yet it was true, I *was* busy: as well as teaching I had residential duties in the school which took up all my time, sometimes until ten or eleven at night. On one Sunday a month, I had to bring the children to Mass in the local parish church. Amazingly, the writer J. R. R. Tolkien attended the same parish. He had retired back to Oxford after his wife's death, and I often saw him sitting in a corner of the church. I wasn't a fan of his longer books, but had always loved *The Hobbit*. I also heard Iris Murdoch talking in the Catholic chaplaincy. After her lecture, a total bore argued some philosophical point with her, ad infinitum, but no matter how irritating he was, she was patient and answered his questions with great respect and humility. I found out later in life that Elizabeth Bowen was another writer who lived nearby in Headington. My fantasy is that I might have got to know her if only I had known this, but I would never have had the courage to knock on her door.

A regret about my time in England is losing touch with people. My mother often quoted the wily Polonius' advice about friends in *Hamlet* to "grapple them to thy soul with hoops of steel." I lost touch with the biology teacher, the music teacher, the games teacher, and Paola, the Italian au pair. She was always desperately homesick for Italy and I had tried to console her, so she invited me back for the summer. First we went to Forte dei Marmi on the Riviera for a week with her rich boyfriend's extended Roman family, which reminded me of the film *Death in Venice*, and, as we sat down to dinner every evening, I fell in love with all things Italian. After a week we went to her more humble hometown on the Adriatic until it was time to return to our jobs in England.

The residential nature of my job was getting me down, as there was no privacy. Then in early 1973 fate intervened, pole-vaulting me out of Oxford. I got viral pneumonia and, finding myself lying Jane Eyre–like in an attic bedroom, went home to recover, staying again with my mother. One day, Charles Merrill, the American editor of the *Arts in Ireland* magazine, rang, asking for Olwyn. She had applied for a job as assistant editor, but had since got another position with which she was happy. I knew she wouldn't want to change.

"She's employed," I said, into the phone.

He sighed in disappointment.

"Eh . . . I'm free," I added on a whim.

"Well . . . I was impressed with her qualifications."

Despite my pass degree, I was given an interview and got the job as assistant editor of the magazine at a starting salary of twenty-five pounds a week which, amazingly, was an average salary then. So I was able to move out of my mother's house to a flat. The Troubles in Northern Ireland were heating up and there was some prejudice against the Irish in England, so I was glad to be back in Dublin. I was also glad to give up teaching, which is a hard job even if it has long holidays. People sometimes don't realize this and complain about teachers having it easy. But the children can be difficult, and you start another day's work of preparation at four or five o'clock when you have spent all day teaching. English is a particularly hard subject too, because of all the marking.

Chapter Twenty-Eight

The magazine job finished in early 1975, so I began freelancing for newspapers, hoping to stay in journalism. One of these was *The Catholic Standard*, where I became friends with the late John Feeney, then the editor, who tried to help me by selling me yet another manual typewriter for ten pounds. He gave me book reviews to write also and, one night in the following summer, sent me to review an O'Casey play, *Behind the Green Curtains*, in the Project Theatre. My old English tutor, Bob Hogan, an eminent O'Casey scholar, was in the audience and we got chatting at the interval. The truth is I was so nervous of standing alone that I latched onto him—it's funny how an aspect of your character can affect your whole life, but as the Greeks said, "Character is fate." I doubt if Bob remembered me, although he said he did. I told him what I'd being doing since college, and he invited me for a drink after the play. "We'll meet under that exit sign," he said. In the pub afterwards we ran into Alan Simpson, the famous Irish director, who talked nonstop about the theater. I remember Bob asked me what I wanted to drink, and I said a glass of lager and lime. He came back with a pint, which impressed me greatly. My expectations must have been low.

Bob was from Missouri but now lived in Delaware, where he was teaching in the state university. He had had a brilliant career and written many books on drama and writing. He told me that he had been separated from his wife for some years. And no, the big American car I had seen back in 1968 wasn't his; he'd had an old banger that year. Afterwards he insisted on walking me home to where I was then living in Sandymount and, although I didn't ask him in, it was the beginning of yet another life. At the time I was sharing a flat with Mary Farl Powers, a willowy beauty, who was the daughter of the American writer J. F. Powers, and herself an established graphic artist. I have good memories of Mary, although many people found her difficult. She had a phobia about television and wouldn't allow one in the flat, but she was kind to me, and later gave the nod of approval to Bob. "He's wiry," she said. Sadly she died of cancer in her forties.

When I met Bob, I had a temporary job in a late-opening gallery, arranged by Mary, and was working most nights, so I missed his many phone calls after our first meeting. He was about to give up, he told me later, but decided to try one more time. On that occasion I remember running into the flat and reaching the phone just before it rang off. By such threads our fates hang. Our first date, a meal out, was unpromising. I felt decidedly uninteresting and didn't know what to talk about. Finally I said that I had promised to visit a friend in Donegal the next weekend. Bob claimed that he was going north also—for research, and could we travel together? What a coincidence, I thought. It never occurred to me that this was probably a ruse. But we took the Donegal bus together and got to know each other on that trip. Bob had just ended another relationship and so had I, so we were both orphans of the storm. We enjoyed being traveling companions and were happy together. The result was that Bob invited me for a vacation to Delaware. The only thing I knew about the state was the popular song "Delaware," with its famous line, "What did Della wear?" I went back to Dublin and packed up my flat. It seemed the right thing to do and it was. I had a feeling that it was meant to be. That all of my previous life had led to this decision.

Around this time I saw Auntie Bronwyn, my father's "other woman," at an art gallery opening. We recognized each other across the room. Out of gaucheness or loyalty to my mother, I didn't speak to her and regret it always. But I felt by the riveted way she stared at me that it must be true about Alistair: I had a half-brother, unseen since childhood. The encounter was the genesis of *Mothers*, my first novel.

I had met Bob again on July 22, 1975, and I went to Delaware three weeks later. I did the same thing as my grandmother and mother: I found love, so I left everything behind. Coincidentally my departure date, August 15, was the anniversary of my grandfather's death forty years previously, and the day my parents became engaged in 1941. I had got to an American university at last—by the back door. Bob lived on campus, so I started continuing education classes in the University of Delaware. At first I couldn't work in the States without a Green Card, so spent my free time sitting out under a tree, or playing tennis in the sun.

I had confided in Bob about my wish to write a novel.

"I don't see you doing it," he said one day.

The truth is I was still afraid to try. So, having no more excuses, I started *Mothers* that September, attending Benedict Kiely's creative writing seminar the following semester—he was a visiting professor in the English Department. At the time abortion rights were in the air, and although my novel was in no way autobiographical, I decided to compare two women of different generations who had the same problem—an unplanned pregnancy to a single woman in a restrictive society. My idea was inspired by the French saying, "Plus ça change, plus c'est la même chose." Bob, a successful playwright, said that three characters would be better, so I added a third. Thanks to him, I discovered that writing is a craft. It's something you learn, although there's also an inborn talent, like being musical. Still the old cliché is true: writing anything is 99 percent perspiration and 1 percent inspiration. It became my passion and something I was meant to do. There is nothing like the happiness of creating something. When I started writing seriously, I finally hooked up with the self I had lost years ago.

Bob was a very positive person, completely unsnobby for a professor and a fan of popular culture, especially comics. He gave me confidence, and I doubt that I would have been a writer without his support. He used to say that this wasn't true, but it is. I never cared about any other critic's opinion because I believed he was a better judge. A writer needs to be around people who will support him or her. It is a lonely road, but no one asks you to travel it, so you can't complain. It's a strange obsession to want to spend your life at a computer. I remember my friend Aisling, the cello player who died young, telling me that she wanted to be a Child of Mary, which was a school sodality, so that her name would be on a board. I suppose writers are the same. They want to be remembered, to make a mark on the cave wall.

Bob helped many people besides me. He was an inspiring teacher, loved by students for his honesty and sense of fun. For me his love was a healing experience. Any relationship takes effort on both sides. Bob referred to ours as "limping along together." I would say that our love grew over the years, rather than being an instant bolt of lightning. It was real, without any fantasy. We got married in 1979 in a register office in Wilmington, "before God and the state of Delaware," after four years of living together. He died in 1999, but it is true that a relationship doesn't end when a person dies, because he is with me every day of my life. But that is leaping into the future, which is now as I write this memoir. This book is the story of my mother and me.

Mothers had been finished in 1978 but, although I sent it out to a few publishers, it lay untouched in a drawer until I was a winner in the first Maxwell House/Arlen House Short Story competition the next year. My winning story, "Underwear," had been inspired by a conversation I had overheard in Bewley's Café about a nun arrested for shoplifting, which I thought said something about Ireland of that time, when change was coming to a rigidly conservative society. Arlen House, a small feminist press, asked if I had any more short stories. I hadn't, but I had written the novel, so they asked to see that and accepted it in late 1979, although it wasn't published until 1982. Everyone has some luck in life and that was mine. My mother had read the typescript and paid me the best compliment ever: "I forgot you wrote it."

She also read an extract from my second novel, *Confessions of a Prodigal Daughter*, which *The Irish Times* had published as a short story. I never liked the title, but the publisher, Marion Boyars, had insisted on it for its suggestion of raciness. The novel opens with a girl shopping with her mother. I had used one of our few rows which took place in St. Stephen's Green when I wanted to buy a five-year diary with a lock and she wanted me to get my hair done. (Nowadays I wonder why I couldn't have bought an ordinary notebook!) The mother's character is heightened to comic effect; while she has aspects of my mother, she is not totally based on her. I had used the same material for a play called *A House for Fools*, which, because it has so many characters, wasn't staged until 2004 by an amateur group.

I was expecting my mother to be angry at my fictional character's similarities to her. I was back from America at the time and she was still living near Ranelagh. She loved going out for morning coffee, so we went to the local pub and I nervously gave her my story. She was in her early sixties then, but old beyond her years because of ill health. She read it silently, her white head bent in concentration. Afterwards she didn't speak.

"You don't like it?" I asked.

"Of course I do! You wrote it."

I took a deep breath. "What is it, then?"

Her blue eyes were mischievous. She folded the newspaper and gave it back to me. "You said you were writing a book about me. This isn't a book."

Had I said that? Perhaps I had said that I was contemplating a novel about a mother/daughter relationship? "It's part of a book," I said, hearing myself add. "I will write a book about you."

She smiled happily. There was a pause. "Just tell me one thing? . . . Did I say that?"

"What?"

"'People will judge you by your underwear.'" It was a line of dialogue from the story. Was she annoyed? Writers are meant to have ice in their veins, but I don't. Before I could reply, my mother sighed. "I must have been drinking. It's not fair to remind me. I hope you haven't told Bob about me."

"Told him what?"

"About my problems."

"Of course I haven't!"

"But this story . . ."

"Mummy, it's fiction!"

She looked at me for a moment. "You know I've always believed in your writing. . . . A writer's capital is her childhood. I gave you that." I was dumbstruck. Other writers have problems with family objections to what they write, but I had got her blessing. She broke the silence. "I want to say . . ." More silence.

"What?"

"I always expected too much of you. . . . You were only a fair-haired child."

"Oh, Mummy . . ."

"I shouldn't have told you everything."

I laughed, surprised. "That was years ago! And there was no one else."

"Children don't owe their parents. It's the other way around."

I did finish that mother/daughter novel, but can barely read it because it is set in St. Patrick's Hospital and seems too literary. I needed more distance from the experience. The characters are Dickensian and the subject matter works better as a play. In the hospital I had met many interesting types and writers use the people they know. My mother was a most quixotic person, so has inspired many of my characters. She had an unusual kindness and once offered hospitality to a stranger she'd met at the bus stop. Another time, a young cousin came to stay with her for a weekend and remained for a whole year—along with a pet parrot, which lived in a cupboard under our stairs. My mother irritated her Clonskeagh neighbors by befriending the Travellers camped by the River Dodder, defending their right to be there and giving parties for their children. She fully accepted Bob as a son-in-law, even though he was a divorced father of five, and took his side if he and I ever had a mild disagreement. She had mellowed about Irish men, but was glad he was American and that I was living in the States. I was following a pattern: my grandmother had gone to America; my mother came back to Ireland; and I had settled in Delaware.

Bob couldn't always see her sense of fun, but she was ill and not at her best by the time they met. And he didn't know the whole story. He used to urge me to "move on," to write about other topics than mothers. But now, over thirty years after her death, I'm still writing about my childhood. I went to a therapist once who told me that we're all unreliable narrators of our own lives: I had wanted my mother to be the best mother in the world so I had invented a myth. But when I told Olwyn this she said that we couldn't all be wrong, we couldn't all be unreliable narrators.

It's the wrong way around when you have to parent your parents, and I won't say it wasn't difficult growing up with two alcoholics, but there are positive aspects to it. For one thing: it makes you more sympathetic. Also, research has shown that the children of alcoholics (COAs, as we are called) sometimes suffer academically but do quite well later in life. If you look at the lives of writers—say Dickens or Joyce, to mention the most famous—many have had insecure childhoods with periods of social embarrassment. There has to be a book in that. What doesn't kill you makes you stronger. "A writer needs as much trauma as he or she can take," according to the late P. D. James.

My mother's good qualities had a big effect on me. Because she loved us, we were able to love. She had been courageous, sending us to college with no money. She taught us resilience and how to survive hard times. She dived into the sea that summer's day in Sandycove, showing no fear. This was her attitude to life and she tried to pass it on to her children. When I complained about moving house so often when we were young, she said, "You'll look back and think: what fun we had!" And I do—almost. I think of my childhood as happy, although my parents' marriage wasn't always so. A married couple needs shared interests. Although never at college, my mother was well-read and often quoted John Donne or Robert Frost, and her liking for Virginia Woolf's *To the Lighthouse* puzzled me as a teenage Brontë fan. My father didn't share my mother's interest in literature. He was meticulously tidy, while she, although a good cook, wasn't. Also, he was calm, while she exploded, particularly when annoyed with him; he was religious, but she wasn't; he was unpunctual, while she was always on time. An F. Scott and Zelda Fitzgerald: they were in love but unsuited, so probably should have married other people. But if they hadn't had their tempestuous life, I wouldn't be here; neither would my brothers and sisters. Both of them loved children and must have had something between them to produce the six of us.

My mother moved house over twenty times in her married life, but always stuck to my father because he needed her. When she went to England, it was out of necessity, and she sent home her salary; our famous London escapade lasted less than a week. In moments of irritation, she claimed that my father had chosen her because she had no near relations, and that he cut her off from her extended Irish family. But the opposite was probably truer. He may have been looked down on by some of her aunts and uncles, or they may have been disappointed at how the marriage had turned out. But she was old enough to have burnt her own milk. Her extended family were bridge-playing sherry-sippers, while my father was the opposite. I was nearly thirty when I bought my first bottle of whiskey on holiday with friends and was shocked at how inexpensive it was—around three or four pounds. I wondered how my father had got through so much money. Was it possible to spend a fortune on drink without killing yourself? "He gambled," my mother sighed. "Didn't you know? I often had wads of cash under my pillow."

After he died, she told me, "I was the only woman who ever loved him."

As a widow, she was in and out of psychiatric hospitals. The troubles of her life had tipped her over the edge. She met only one sympathetic doctor, who ran a program for alcoholics on Dublin's north side. Thanks to him, she limped along, treading water for long stretches. Her illness had made her do crazy things: write outlandish letters, spend wildly, drink, disappear. I once read an article in a magazine about bipolar disease. The symptoms could have been my mother's, yet she was never correctly diagnosed. Her prescribed antidepressants were not helpful. Nowadays there are mood stabilizers and the outlook is better. I spoke to a psychiatrist recently who told me that the disorder was not commonly diagnosed in the 1960s and that my mother's mental state might have been triggered by amphetamine use, which she took to stay awake when nursing. Another symptom of bipolar disease is that you think you are an important person. My mother never thought that she was, but she identified with Jackie Kennedy and wore the same ocelot coat. Clothes were very important to her. In college I was beautifully dressed, but often had no bus fare.

There is now research that bereavement in childhood can affect mental health in adulthood. My mother lost her mother when she was sixteen months old. Along with her two siblings, she had become emotionally disturbed. Life evolves from what went before, so is it too far-fetched to think that loss in one generation can be passed to another? Can suffering change our DNA?

According to Philip Roth, when a writer is born into a family, it's the end of the family. But a memoir also gives it an afterlife. Hamlet instructed Horatio: "draw thy breath in pain / To tell my story" and that's what I've tried to do for my mother. Her life affected me, but for the better because I was determined not to end up in another psychiatric hospital. It's a useful thing to have your midlife crisis early and get it out of the way. But my mother never recovered from her childhood. She was always insecure and unable to separate from her own children when the time came. Her habit of disappearing usually happened when she had taken a drink. Once she was discovered sitting weeping on the steps of 43 Pembroke Road, the Victorian house where she had been born. The present-day tenant found her and drove her home.

I never pass that house without stopping. A few years ago Olwyn and I were shown around by a builder who was converting it. We were looking through the railings when he invited us in. Surrounded by ghosts, we stood in the old-world basement kitchen. It had probably not changed since the days when my mother and her siblings played there. An original mantelpiece and the remains of a chandelier were in the upstairs drawing room. Reaching back into the past, I could almost smell the flowers with which my grandmother was said to have filled her house.

"It was a house that loved children," Aunt Noreen had told me, when I pressed her for information. "Your grandmother was soft, unlike the other members of her family," she added. But Noreen was unsentimental about Donal, the child who had died on his First Communion Day. "He was spoiled," she said, "used to people calling him 'pretty Donal.' When that stopped he went around complaining, 'No one say pretty Donal.'" It became a family saying. Yet Noreen had christened her own son the same name.

Donal and his mother were equally victims of World War I, as if they had been in the trenches, she also said. Although we were always told that they died of the black flu, which had spread from the continent in those years, it was typhoid fever, according to Noreen. The account of their deaths sounds like something out of *East Lynne*, with a mother promising to follow a dying child into eternity, but that's how stories get handed down in families. At my own first communion, I met the Jesuit uncle who had told Donal that he was dying. His words had made the child hysterical with fear and he begged his mother to come with him. If her child hadn't been upset, my grandmother might not have tempted fate by promising to go.

When she died, my grandmother entered into myth. Her wonky samovar, now in my garage, survived our many house moves. It was a prop for one of her and my grandfather's early films, although I don't know which one. Recently, academic experts in Irish film studies have contacted me about my grandmother's role as a film producer and possible scriptwriter of *Knocknagow*. She was the main investor in the Film Company of Ireland but, like many women, she has been written out of history. Her home at 43 Pembroke Road is now in Celtic Tiger flats, with the gates governed by remote control. The stone eagle still guarding the hall door couldn't keep fate at bay but, although I know nothing about the age of trees, the big chestnut in the front garden could have been there in 1919. Other families have grandmothers. We never knew ours, but she left us something: a sense of loss, which my mother never recovered from. It shows you never escape from a family's love, even by death.

When I was home from Delaware, my mother had a habit of ringing me and saying things like, "Be sure to have a party when I die."

"But you're not dying."

She sighed. "I hope there'll be enough money."

"You're only sixty-three. You need to eat properly, that's all—fruit and porridge."

"Have some sense! I can't live on fruit!"

I knew she had a bad heart, but felt safe because she had never had a heart attack. There would surely be some warning. But I was probably in denial about her health, which is usually the case with close relatives.

Soon after that, Olwyn gave a party in her flat. It was on Easter Saturday and my mother, who couldn't bear to be left out of anything, phoned in the middle of it, asking how to cook a chicken. Olwyn was mildly irked that she couldn't entertain her friends without my mother butting in. So I ended up sitting on the stairs, chatting to her on the phone for hours. She was in a weird prophetic mood. It was a change because, although she told endless stories, she had never previously confided in me about missing her mother. Now she did.

"The loss affected your whole life," I said.

"People said it couldn't have . . . because I never knew her." She paused, falling into a silence. "That always hurt me."

"They were talking rubbish. Of course you missed her!"

"There's something else."

"What is it?" I said.

"I never liked my father."

I was surprised—she had always praised him to us. "But you can't like everyone."

In all our difficulties, my grandfather had been a role model, the good example, whose achievements we had to emulate. He had had four careers: journalist, criminal lawyer, American diplomat, and pioneering film producer. My mother had always claimed that her childhood was happy. What was she saying now? One thing had always puzzled me: my grandfather had come from humble beginnings. He knew the value of education, yet he had discouraged my mother and her sister from going to college: Auntie Ellen had won a scholarship to Ursuline College in New Orleans, but her father urged her to marry a charming womanizer instead; my mother wasn't encouraged to study either, although she was clever. It was the fate of women then. This was probably why my mother had pushed us into third level education.

"He wasn't a good father," she went on.

"What do you mean?"

"He said terrible things to my brother Stephen." My mother hesitated. "That he'd lost a good son and was left with a delinquent."

For years, there was a photo of Stephen in military school uniform on our mantelpiece. After his mother's death, he fell into the fire while playing Blind Man's Buff at a party. He was given morphine for pain, which caused him problems in later life when he had kidney problems. When he was given painkillers, it was a key fitting a lock, my mother told me.

Then she told me how she had discovered that Stephen had become an addict. Her Jesuit uncle, a pious man with a reputation for retreats, had written to her that he had "good news about Stephen." My mother had hurried to see him, but instead of good news learned that her brother was to have a lobotomy. It was a barbaric operation, done at the time to cure mental problems, but has been totally discredited. Bizarrely, the doctor who invented it won the Nobel Prize for Medicine in 1949. I tried to console my mother that day, but the memory always upset her. Her brother's emotions were flattened by the operation, and he spent the rest of his life in a Brooklyn veterans' hospital. It was the last talk we had because she died in her sleep the next night. She was found dead in the early morning of Easter Monday.

In 1981, Bob and I had bought a small house in Rathmines in south Dublin and within walking distance of my mother's home. I had expected to see more of her, since we were planning to live half the year in Ireland and half in Delaware. We had just moved into our house when friends arrived to tell me the bad news—we had no phone, like half the country then—so I thought they were delivering furniture and began to thank them.

"Your mother has died," they said.

"W-What?" I couldn't take it in. She and I would never be able to talk again, and this time she had left for good.

I couldn't look at her dead body, but Barry identified it and later gave me her wedding ring and Mater Hospital badge, of which she had been so proud. A few neighbors and cousins came to her funeral in Milltown parish church and her old friend Father F. X. Martin did the honors. Because of my grandfather's 1916 imprisonment, Garda Outriders escorted her body to Glasnevin where we laid her beside my father.

Goodnight, sleep well, loved and loving mother.

As we walked away from the grave, an older cousin reminisced, smiling. "Your mother was gay in the old meaning of the word. One day she was minding us as children—I can still see her, sitting on a rock in wildest Connemara, painting her toenails red. There was no one to see them for miles around."

That was my mother.

Epilogue

When 4 Myrtle Avenue, Dún Laoghaire was for sale about fifteen years ago, I couldn't miss the chance to view it. Olwyn, who has become an advocate for the mentally ill, had founded a housing fellowship that provides flats for those leaving hospital with nowhere to live. That day she was looking for a property with conversion possibilities, and the large semi-detached was in the right catchment area. I really wanted her to buy it, even if it was for the fellowship, believing it would somehow make up for the losses of our past. In my favorite novel, *The Mill on the Floss*, the brother Tom buys back the mill that the family had lost in childhood due to their father's mismanagement. We had never owned this house but had spent formative years there. It seemed like a long time, but it was only thirty-three months. As well as Dubber, Myrtle Avenue has often entered my dreams, probably because early adolescence is etched so strongly in memory.

We arrived before the agent and waited in the car outside. The front garden was now even more overgrown than in our day. Like the other four houses in the row, it had been newly built in the 1950s, but was now neglected compared to its well-kept neighbors. It needed a coat of paint and a down-pipe dangled like a broken limb.

I shivered, remembering the cold of the past. In the days before insulation and central heating, the walls hadn't even been properly plastered. Yet, at the time, the house had seemed the last word in modernity. But we hadn't high expectations for comfort then: we were just happy to be together. I sat there thinking: if we could get back to the past, what would we change about our lives? Probably nothing. We wouldn't exchange our own sorrows for the joys of the whole world. I had read a poem somewhere expressing these sentiments.

I stared at the field opposite. "Remember the hockey on Saturdays?"

"I'd forgotten that," my sister said.

Shouts of triumph and despair rang again in my ears: the clash of sticks, then the pant and pound of grown men running. Now trees grew in the field and a man played ball with his dog. In the old days it was just grass, a reminder of the North Dublin countryside which we had forsaken.

My sister dragged me back from the past. "The roof's iffy."

I peered upwards—there was moss on the chimney and grass grew in the gutters. "It needs a few slates."

At last the agent came and fiddled with the lock. "These should be the right keys."

The door was stiff, but he pushed it open.

"It hasn't changed much," I said, following him inside.

While he showed my sister around, I lingered in the hall. Amazingly, the maroon Tintawn carpet my parents had bought was still on the stairs. Over half a century had passed, but the walls had the same icy pink and lemon washes. Only the sitting room had been papered over, and there were ugly DIY insulating tiles dangling from the ceiling. Nothing had been done to the kitchen with its standalone sink, and the taps that sometimes gave us slight electric shocks were the same. At the time no one worried about this phenomenon, but the memory made me afraid to try them now. "Don't touch it! I'll put on the kettle," I heard my father say, as his ghost came into the kitchen, as usual sartorially dressed. My mother, wearing an apron, hurriedly prepared the evening meal. "I'll get on to the landlord," she said.

The 1950s kitchen presses were intact, and the same hatch opened into the dining room. I had done my homework there, sitting at the oval mahogany table, learning speeches from Shakespeare or Latin verb endings. My mother's voice now called in my head for me to bring in the washing from the line, which was always my job. So I went out the drawing room French doors, leading to the back garden. There was no clothesline now, and just a jungle for a garden. In the past, mating cats had wailed there nightly, reminding me of crying babies.

Olwyn and the estate agent stayed in the back garden, looking up at the roof. I went upstairs, other memories flooding in: my father's illness; our mother's departure; our things being put on the side of the road while we waited for the movers. My parents' bedroom was huge and looked out to a balcony. Mine looked smaller—a consequence of my being bigger perhaps. I stood at the door remembering the summer nights when I had read by candlelight, after we returned from walking the pier with our father. I was both happy and unhappy; I missed my mother terribly. "Don't go on about things!

I came back, didn't I?" her voice now said in my head. "You did," I whispered. "You always came back."

Despite my *The Mill on the Floss* fantasies of regaining our old home, my sister didn't buy it. The house wasn't suitable for flats, and there was something wrong with the drains. I was disappointed, but you cannot step in the same stream twice. That day I was surrounded by ghosts: my parents, the Fergusons, and the stamp dealer Dr. Singer. He had been released from prison because a member of the jury had lost money in the scam. Dr. Singer could still be alive in Canada, but the old people would have been dead for years. How long had they remained living next door, pottering around in their garden, before going to nursing homes? Were they really that old? They had seemed ancient to me, but young people have no sense of age. I didn't think so at the time, but my parents weren't old when we left the house—my mother forty-one and my father fifty-two. Who had lived there after us? It must have been someone who couldn't afford a new carpet, by the look of things. The landlord had done nothing in our day and obviously nothing since.

Finally I joined my sister in the garden where a gull had landed on the path, reminding me of the sea and the day of my mother's famous swim. Again I heard the waves breaking against the sea wall and the plop as she dived in and disappeared out to sea. I thought that she'd drown that day, but she didn't. According to a Robert Graves poem there is one story and one story only, and my mother's voice reminded me again: "A writer's capital is her childhood. I gave you yours." It was a license to write this memoir, which among other things, has been an attempt to bring her back.

About the Author

Mary Rose Callaghan is the author of nine novels, including *A Bit of a Scandal,* (2009), *Billy, Come Home* (2007), *The Visitors' Book* (2001), and *Emigrant Dreams* (1996). As well as writing for periodicals, she has published *Kitty O'Shea, A Life of Katharine Parnell* (1989) which was republished twice. She has been assistant editor of, and has written thirty articles for, *The Dictionary of Irish Literature* (1979, 1996), edited by the late Robert Hogan, and has broadcast stories on BBC radio. She lived for many years in Newark, Delaware, where she taught classes at the university, but now lives in County Wicklow, Ireland.

Lightning Source UK Ltd.
Milton Keynes UK
UKHW01n2103160518
322713UK00001B/53/P